Trees in the Forest

Growing Readers and Writers
through
Deep Comprehension

Rita Cevasco, MA, SLP

with Tracy Molitors

Illustrated by Tracy Molitors

Crooked Tree Press • Cincinnati

ISBN 978-0-9979031-1-9

Library of Congress Control Number: 2016953418

Printed in the United States of America.

Published by Crooked Tree Press. To learn more about the book or its authors, visit www.rootedinlanguage.com.

The images in this book are reproductions of original watercolors by Tracy Molitors, www.tracymolitors.com.

To our husbands, Rick Cevasco and Tom Molitors, who support us in all things and in all ways.

To our children—Ian, Emma, Zach, Moira, David, Claire and Vincent—who continually teach us that we are not as smart as we think—a healthy lesson, indeed!

—R.C. and T.M.

"Something so hard can be so easy if you just have a little help. In the right place, under the right conditions, you can finally stretch out into what you're supposed to be."

—from *Lab Girl* by Hope Jahren

Preface

From the first moment I heard Peter Bower's expression "Study the trees to learn the forest," the metaphor resonated with me. During the course of 30 years as a speech-language pathologist, reading and writing instructor, and mother, I have built my life around helping children learn necessary skills (trees) in order to be successful in the bigger world of literacy (forest). I've seen firsthand how important it is to help children communicate, engage in the reading world, reach their best writing potential, and believe in their own ability to learn. Mastering language in all its forms—listening, speaking, reading, and writing—is not optional. It's a life changer.

I have borrowed and expanded the metaphor of the tree and forest for this book. The Language Tree (page 75) is my representation of how the different areas of language arts study (such as phonics and grammar) tap into skill sets children need in order to grow as readers and writers. Helping children nourish the roots of their learning leads to stronger language skills overall.

This book marks the beginning of a long exploratory journey investigating the Language Tree. In it, I share concepts with you that I have taught children and their parents over the years and strategies that help kids move along a path to becoming stronger readers and writers. I share my thoughts regarding the relationship between reading, writing, and all other language skills, as well as ideas taught in my online Brave Writer class, called "Foundations in Writing," and in my reading curriculum, the *Wand*. These ideas can grow literacy in all of us.

We cannot separate reading from writing—these two branches of language are entwined and must grow together. I love the phrase "roots entwined" from the poem by Pablo Neruda. The image of roots entwined suggests entities so interconnected that they cannot be separated.

I've heard the phrase applied to the parent-child bond. The metaphor also works to describe children's reading and writing skills, interwoven within their underlying language skills. The image of roots entwined also reminds us that children learn best in caring and encouraging relationships. My goal is to help parents understand that the loving responsiveness that fostered their children's speaking skills is the same approach needed to foster all areas of language growth. We want kids to work to a level of success. Children learn more from their successes than their failures. This is when kids have the ah-ha moments. This is when children learn how to learn.

More than anything we want to give kids the courage to read and write, to see themselves differently, to believe that they are readers and writers. This is my goal for all children, not just my students who have dyslexia, dysgraphia, or challenges related to comprehension or expressive language. All children benefit from meaningful strategies that connect their skills (trees) to their more complex language thinking systems (forests).

Many children who struggle get stuck in their learning, becoming frustrated, wanting to give up, or worse, secretly wondering if they are not smart enough. My goal is to help kids move along a path, figure out what is blocking their way, and then guide them to the next step, and the next, and the next—all while helping them to better appreciate the value and joy of sharing their ideas with others.

Throughout this book, I will use the phrase *struggling readers and writers*. I witness the challenges that some children (including my students) face in their school days, every day. They and their parents need help and encouragement, rather than pretending that all is well when they know better. Therefore, describing some children as *struggling readers and writers* is to acknowledge within these pages the impact learning challenges can have on school, family, and relationships.

I owe a debt of gratitude to all the mentors and educators who have shared ideas with me. Many of the strategies I share here were presented at conferences, discussed over lunches, or passed on secondhand by colleagues. I cannot begin to credit the originators of these strategies or trace the ways they have morphed over the decades. Even my original ideas have roots in others' work. In addition, hundreds of my students and their parents have brought me to a level of insight and understanding that no college course could ever teach. My own children have as well. We who teach reading and writing have all shared our ideas and learned together. This book is an extension of that worthy endeavor.

There is a learning model in education: *I do it. We do it. You do it.* This means: I will show you. We will do it together. Then you will be able to do it independently. For most of us, the pattern is actually: *I do it. We do it. We do it. We do it. We do it...* and onward, depending on your child's need for support... until finally, *You do it.* In this book, we will engage in the activities together, giving you the confidence and understanding to *do it* with your kids.

Therefore, **Trees in the Forest** is organized to teach you, the parent, important concepts and strategies. I have asked a parent and her children to join me in this venture, so that you can see how learning unfolds. In addition, I want you to experience learning the same strategies your children will be learning—exploring ideas and growing *yourself* as a reader and a writer.

I invited my friend and artist, Tracy Molitors, to join us. She illustrated the concepts in this book and shares her watercolor trees throughout these pages. Tracy taught art to my children because I was intimidated by the thought of exploring art with them. Learning with Tracy helped me grow in my love for art. She also helped me realize how much language can be enriched by art. As my children learned with Tracy, so did I, becoming more comfortable holding a sketch pad and pencil. This is the beauty of learning with our children—it ignites our own discovery and passion. The more passion we feel, the better teachers we become. The more we connect to our children's learning, the better parents we become. The more we grow, the better people we become.

—Rita

"...being able to derive happiness from discovery is a recipe for a beautiful life."

—from *Lab Girl* by Hope Jahren

Contents

Introduction

Imagine the forest is the world of words…

Each tree is a separate skill to learn or a piece of literature to study. It is a world where our children happily run from tree to tree, comfortable in this forest of reading and writing. They are at home under its canopy and know how to navigate its paths. Our children are the rangers who not only understand the forest terrain, they cultivate its growth.

From Nemo's Journal:

"I wanted to hand feed a bird because I am curious how its tiny feet feel… It was very hard to stand still. Finally, when the Chickadee arrived it looked like a dropping black and white marble as it descended on my hand."

–Nemo, age 10

In Nemo's journal we find the kind of writing moments we wait for: moments when our children write a sentence that gives us pause—to laugh, to ponder, to marvel.

Our kids often *speak* delightful adages. My daughter, at a young age, proclaimed in annoyance: "Toilets should not have minds of their own!" Tracy's son, as a young sage, noted: "Some days you just chew gum." We families savor our favorite quips. Yet, when our kids' shining insights show up in their writing, it is a special delight. Funny or wise, kind or sarcastic, their perceptions are the crowning glory of all our teaching efforts.

When I first met Nemo, pictured opposite, he was beginning to enjoy writing but did not like reading. He loved to talk but did not understand the rules of dialogue. Since entering the world of text, where he has learned to appreciate the words of others and write his own, Nemo has grown in his ability to engage. He is also an insightful writer.

Not all children struggle with learning, but all children struggle with writing. Even the loved-the-pen-from-the-moment-I-held-it-writers must learn to write well. Words are revised again and again in order to write clear thoughts. Insight comes with wandering, discovery, and reexamination, and this takes time.

We don't need our children to be perfect writers, but we want their writing to bring forth their grace-filled moments, as Nemo did. Moments we see when they converse, or argue, or hang out with friends. We want them to walk the forest path—from verbal skills to writing skills. We want to make space for their thoughts to land on paper in a lovely, yet coherent way—*like a tiny Chickadee, dropping like a black and white marble in their hands.*

Of equal importance, we want to cultivate our own relationship with words, our own path in the forest, so that we, too, become rangers who appreciate and support new growth.

I have been witness to grace-filled writing moments—with my own children and my students, even those who struggle with reading and writing. I have had a few grace-filled moments of my own and read grace-filled lines in wonderful pieces of literature.

Shining moments cannot be commanded. Too much direction and we get excellent mechanics without a soul, much like a piano student who masters intricate finger-work without inspiring a listener's emotional response. Instead, we want to become students of the forest along with our children. Language arts is not an untamed wilderness, but an inviting, tree-lined trail. It is a path to growing our children's language skills, so that as their skills grow, the writing soil is tilled and enriched. As their skills grow, shining moments shoot out of the ground, tall and unexpected.

If you take this journey with me, you will understand how this path of language discovery—with our attention to strengthening skills—will open to a field of writing. As we travel, we will understand the terrain well enough to anticipate missteps and enjoy the adventure.

Throughout this book you'll find insights from three voices of experience:

✳ I share writing samples from other adults and children, personal thoughts in **Rita's Journal**, and knowledge in **Connecting Language to Language Arts**.

✳ Tracy Molitors, illustrator and art teacher, shares thoughts in **Tracy's Journal** and ideas about art in **Connecting Art to Language Arts**.

✳ **Laurie's Journal** offers the perspective of a homeschool parent and shares some of the work of her children, Nemo and Sigourney.

We use three works of literature for the activities in this book:

✳ *The Invention of Wings* by Sue Monk Kidd

✳ *This Is Not My Hat* by Jon Klassen

✳ *Blart—A Little Blob of Art* by Tracy Molitors

Connecting Art to Language Arts ✕ Uniting Fields of Study

The pairing of two disciplines, such as art and language arts, can yield opportunities for deeper understanding. I find that when I draw and write together, I feel greater connection and empathy with my subject.

I experienced the value of connection in a class combining figure drawing with martial arts and boxing. This pairing startles people when I first mention it, but it was an eye-opening example of how we can cultivate skills by uniting fields of study. At one point, we closed our eyes, *feeling* rather than *watching* our way through a pose. We paired our body movement with blind contour drawing—looking only at our subject, not the drawing we were creating. Our physical experience increased our sensitivity and insight.

Later, after practicing movements from kung fu, muay Thai, and karate, we attempted to draw a figure in some of our earlier poses. It was as if the drawing came from inside as well as outside. My connection with the position was so much deeper that it influenced not only my basic knowledge of the pose, but the very quality of the line I drew.

Pairing art with language arts, while not so unexpected, still inspires us to explore reading and writing with new eyes. This pairing does not require any advanced skill, or indeed, any skill at all. (You should have seen my attempts at kung fu.) Rather, all we need is the willingness to take a risk and explore a new approach.

—Tracy

Laurie's Journal

I wish there were an adult class to climb the tree before we sit down at it with our children. We parents are so afraid to miss something, so unsure of ourselves. I realize what I really want is a forest guide.

I love all of this—working with our children is an excuse to poke into the corners of our own wonder and build it slowly from the ground up, reminding me of how important it is to go slower and deeper.

Trees in the Forest

Study the trees to learn the forest.

—Peter Bowers

As we begin our journey through the world of words—all the books written and the papers yet to come—we adults are already deep in the woods as readers and writers. We might love the woods or dread guiding our children down its path. Still, we long to deepen our family's connection to the trees.

So here we are. We carry a backpack filled with language arts programs, book lists, and a read-aloud or two. Our children carry their own packs: the young with phonics books and early readers, the older ones with pens and papers, spelling lists, a classic novel long overdue at the library.

We stop to admire a particular tree—some lovely work of literature—sitting together under its canopy and opening our packs. We have been told that by visiting these trees and engaging with our language arts programs, our children will become avid readers and insightful writers. We hope that with effective use of the items in our packs, our children will be able to create little saplings of their own.

But after a few years of visiting these literary trees, their connection to the items in their backpacks feels distant. We wonder how we can help our children use the items in their backpacks effectively. Have we chosen the right programs? Are there enough of them? Do our kids actually learn from these programs, or are they just carrying them around?

Peter Bowers, quoted earlier, shared the metaphor that if we study a single tree, we can learn the forest. But what does it mean to study a **Tree**, and what does it mean to learn the **Forest**? The Tree is a metaphor for deep learning in one *area of study* in order to gain understanding and competency within our world of words. The Forest is a metaphor for this vast network of reading and writing.

Here are some analogies to help us distinguish a **Tree** from a **Forest**, as related to language arts study:

Tree	**is to**	**Forest**	**as...**
single skill	is to	passage	
passage	is to	book	
book	is to	literature	

The Tree to Forest analogy is, after all, how language works. A young toddler's first word teaches her about the world of words, igniting exponential growth in vocabulary within a few months. Her first two-word utterance sparks an explosion of sentences within a year. Between the ages of 12 months and 5 years, a child's entire spoken language system has emerged and formed all its necessary structural elements.

In this same way, growth occurs with reading and writing, from first words to sentences to paragraphs to books, only the process is more complex, sometimes labored, and is cultivated slowly over many decades. The entire language system is a vast and incredible network: a living Forest with entwined roots, running sap, veined leaves, and limitless rings of knowledge.

To cultivate this Forest, we need to study many Trees. We will need to nurture different skills along the way, including:

- Comprehension
- Phonics and spelling
- Handwriting, cursive, and keyboarding
- Vocabulary and word study
- Grammar and punctuation

This book starts us on a journey to be *intentional*, studying Deep Meaning and Comprehension. Meaning is the essence of why we use language—what we share and why it matters. Meaning is the essence of reading and writing, as well.

On this journey, we are going to study a few trees together for a deeper understanding of text. Because we want to facilitate our children's learning, we will do these activities ourselves, improving our own understanding, thus laying a path for our children's growth in reading and writing.

We will unearth what literature has to teach us, exploring samples of writing to learn the world of writing. We will uncover the relationship between the roots and the canopy, between strengthening skills and appreciating literature. Only then will we share our discoveries with our children.

So drop your backpacks. Let's climb a tree together.

First Tree

Capturing Thoughts: Conversations with Text

Writers choose words carefully to convey meaning.

In fiction, the writer crafts characters, plotlines, conflicts, and interactions in order to convey not just a story, but also deep messages. Strong writers reveal meaning by engaging the reader in a relationship.

Think of someone you know intimately—a spouse, a parent, a friend, a sibling, a child.

Imagine you are spending a day together, sometimes talking, and sometimes just sharing the same space. In intimate relationships, we move in synchrony, conveying ongoing messages passed without words: through a look, body position, eye contact, sighs, and movements. The greater the intimacy, the more likely these unspoken thoughts will be noticed, shared, and most importantly, correctly interpreted.

As a writer, I hope to develop a kind of intimacy with the reader through my writing **On the Page**. As a reader, I approach the text with my own experience and knowledge and create a response **In My Head**. The better my writing, the more I evoke interpretive thoughts in the reader. The better my reading skills, the more I receive a writer's intended message and engage in interpretive thinking.

Learning to look closely at text, to find passages worth discussing, and to engage with the words, are necessary ingredients in studying a Tree to learn the Forest. Educators call this practice *Close Reading*. [See Connecting Language to Language Arts: Close Reading.]

One way to look closely at text is through *copywork*. Copywork is the practice of carefully transcribing the writer's words using our best handwriting. Copywork requires coordination of many details in writing: grammatical structure, word choice, spelling, punctuation, and of course, meaning. This list is complex and demanding, tapping abilities which may still be developing. Children are busy mastering individual skills, so coordination of their achievements develops over time, especially in their original writing.

When we develop activities from a copywork passage to help our children practice writing proficiently, we engage in what I call **Intentional Copywork**. Intentional Copywork includes deep exploration of each area of language arts: comprehension; phonics and spelling; handwriting, cursive, and keyboarding; vocabulary and word study; and grammar and punctuation. These skills, needed for original writing, are best practiced in writing that does not also demand creative expression. Instead, each language arts specialty is analyzed within a passage, practiced separately, and finally, practiced in consolidation with all other skills in copywork writing.

Intentional Copywork improves our ability to look deeply at meaning within text—both the words On the Page and the thoughts those words evoke In My Head. The idea of separating the words On the Page from those In My Head helps us to become more observant of both the writer and ourselves. Our interactions build intimacy with writing and with reading, helping us to connect one to the other.

Connecting Language to Language Arts ✴ Close Reading

Since *Close Reading* became an educational mandate, a new Frankenstein's monster has been created for both teachers and students. By quantifying and measuring abstract thinking, the Close Reading movement conveys the message to kids that there are only right answers to be found within text.

Close Reading is evolving into more than the ability of a reader to comprehend both the literal and implied meanings of a text. That is a fine goal. My traditional school students now have to notice and understand *rhetorical devices* used by the writer. And they have to understand the word *rhetorical*, which seems to be a shape-shifting piece of jargon.

But wait, there's more… Close Reading also asks children to notice the writing structure and its purpose in driving the story.

Still more… Children are asked to analyze the writer's grammatical style and its effectiveness. In addition, students must evaluate the writer's word choice.

Tired yet? Close Reading involves ferreting out hidden bias. Students must not only identify genre, but now must determine how genre selection impacts theme.

Should we stop now? In other words, the Close Reading monster asks kids as young as elementary school age to use the level of challenging analysis that my daughter faced as a college English major!

Close Reading should be an act of discovery on the part of the growing reader, taking years to fully develop. Unfortunately, with complex abstract analysis being quantified in schools across the nation, deep reading is being reduced to a rubric. An elaborate five-course meal, which should be slowly savored and enjoyed, has been mass produced into fast food.

Let's encourage children's understanding and connection with text in a way that inspires their love for reading.

Deep meaning and understanding happens best through time, exploration, and discovery, in settings rich in conversation and shared experience. More than anything, children need time—decades in fact—to learn how to mull over a book, spend a week on a passage, play with ideas, and create new worlds along with a writer's.

To think deeply we need to explore deeply. To read "closely" we need to feel close to the reading experience.

—Rita

Let's begin by exploring our relationship with the writer. We will climb the tree *The Invention of Wings* by Sue Monk Kidd. This is the first of many activities we adults practice, preparing us to lead our children toward deep meaning and comprehension. Because we want to explore our connection with the writer, this exercise is best performed if you have read or are reading the book. Let's look at a passage in which a young enslaved girl, Hetty, is going about her daily chores.

The Invention of Wings by Sue Monk Kidd

Character: Hetty

I walked back past the stable and carriage house. The path took me cross the whole map of the world I knew. I hadn't yet seen the spinning globe in the house that showed the rest of it. I poked along, wishing for the day to get used up so me and mauma could go to our room. It sat over the carriage house and didn't have a window. The smell of manure from the stable and the cow house rose up there so ripe it seemed like our bed was stuffed with it instead of straw. The rest of the slaves had their rooms over the kitchen house.

The wind whipped up and I listened for ship sails snapping in the harbor cross the road, a place I'd smelled on the breeze, but never seen. The sails would go off like whips cracking and all us would listen to see was it some slave getting flogged in a neighbor-yard or was it ships making ready to leave. You found out when the screams started up or not.

The sun had gone, leaving a puckered place in the clouds, like the button had fallen off. I picked up the battling stick by the wash pot, and for no good reason, jabbed it into a squash in the vegetable garden. I pitched the butternut over the wall where it splatted in a loud mess.

Then the air turned still. Missus' voice came from the back door, said, "Aunt-Sister, bring Hetty in here to me right now."

I went to the house, thinking she was in an uproar over her squash. I told my backside to brace up.

Connecting Language to Language Arts ✹ Engaging with Text

As I read the excerpt from *The Invention of Wings*, I immediately begin to translate the writer's words into my own thoughts, connecting ideas with what I know of the world, history, and human nature. In order to join in relationship with the writer, I have to allow what is In My Head to be noticed (by me) and contemplated (again, by me).

We all gather meaning when reading, to one degree or another, and there is no right or wrong way to engage or interpret text, as long as we do engage. For instance, when I read the following passage, I infer that Hetty has lived her entire life within the confines of the property.

> I walked back past the stable and carriage house. The path took me cross the whole map of the world I knew.

This is one level of engagement with the writer, in which I interpret the words to glean the underlying message.

If I allow myself greater intimacy with the text, which may not happen with every book, I allow my thoughts to evoke feelings, such as sadness that Hetty is a prisoner, and the reminder that all forms of slavery are prisons.

If I allow myself intimacy with the writer, not just the text, I may begin to think about Sue Monk Kidd's voice and style. I may attend to her word choice and structure, in appreciation of her writing craft. If I feel a kinship with this writer, I may pause to enjoy the metaphor Kidd crafted: that Hetty's yard is like an entire world to her. I may appreciate that by comparing Hetty's movements within the yard to a map of her existence, Kidd inspires a visual image of smallness and physical limitation.

Did I think all these things when I first read Kidd's book? Probably not, but when I engaged in Intentional Copywork, more thoughts developed In My Head.

—Rita

It is tempting when practicing this exercise to wonder if we will know the right answers, but it is not about right answers. Instead, the goal is to engage. There is a saying about marriage: "It's not about being right; it's about being relational!" This is true of engaging with text: it's not about thinking the right thoughts; it's about being relational with the text and the writer, allowing our thoughts to emerge and be noticed.

The reader reads messages on two levels:

1. The overt message conveyed by the words On the Page

2. The covert message buried beneath or hidden within the words, emerging as thoughts In My Head

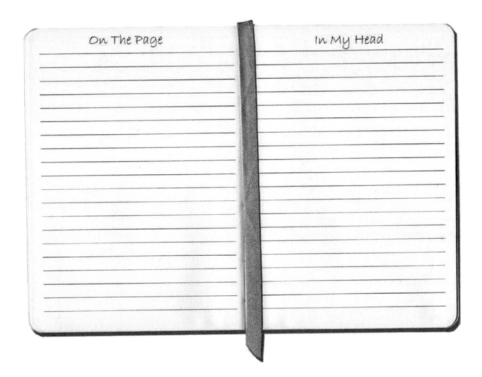

The activity in this lesson is called **On the Page/ In My Head.** In this activity, we copy the writer's words on the left side of the page, and our own interpretations and thoughts on the right side of the page. This helps us acknowledge that writers use words to convey both overt and covert messages.

We copy the passage in sections, remembering to stop and capture the thoughts In My Head. Complete the passage, writing portions of text first on the left side of your journal page (or use the one we have provided in Appendix A), then interpretive thoughts on the right side. There's no need to write complete sentences for In My Head thoughts; just try to capture ideas. Here is my sample:

On The Page	In My Head
I walked back past the stable and carriage house. The path took me cross the whole map of the world I knew. I hadn't yet seen the spinning globe in the house that showed the rest of it. I poked along, wishing for the day to get used up so me + mauma could go to our room. It sat over the carriage house and didn't have a window. The smell of manure from the stable + the cow house rose up there so ripe it seemed like our bed was stuffed with it instead of straw. The rest of the slaves had their rooms over the kitchen house.	• she had never left the property — maybe never even out front of the house? • not educated • not allowed in some rooms either → a long + tedious day (days!) • only 1 room to call her own Disgusting! Yet, she prefers that room to life outside the room. Refuge! • overbearing smell • over kitchen — better smells, but hot!
The wind whipped up and I listened for ship sails snapping in the harbor cross the road, a place I'd smelled on the breeze, but never saw. The sails would go off like whips cracking + all us would listen to see was it some slave getting flogged in a neighbor-yard. You found out when the screams started up or not.	• So close to the ocean, yet never saw it • Trapped in a walled yard • Not unusual to hear screams — Frightening + horrible to hear human cries of pain!

Rita's Journal

*To demonstrate the validity of various interpretations, I gave my passage to my book club members, six women whom I have known for many years. We call ourselves the "All Talk At Once" book club, so this was a rare moment of quiet as they engaged in the **On the Page/ In My Head** exercise. I enjoyed the similarities and differences in how intimately each person engaged, as well as their differences in interpretation, especially from my own. You will find some examples of the book club responses in Appendix C.*

"Full ownership of a book only comes when you have made it a part of yourself."

—From *How to Read a Book* by Mortimer Adler

Parent Copywork ✺ On the Page/ In My Head

Here are explicit instructions to reference when using this exercise with your children:

*Everyone has different experiences with this exercise of **On the Page/ In My Head**. You may think of relating with text as a habit you take for granted or you may discover this is a new skill to master.*

*As you do your copywork, you are going to separate your writing into two columns. On the left side, you will first copy the passage—the words on the page, verbatim. We call this side **On the Page**, and it is typical copywork.*

Once you have completed a section of the copywork on the left side, stopping at a natural break in the passage, you will then proceed to the right side of the paper. In this column, you will write the messages and clues the writer is conveying to you. You will interpret the meaning of this portion of the passage, as well as your own thoughts, reactions, and feelings.

*Continue copying the passage **On the Page**, one portion at a time. At the end of each section, stop and capture your thoughts **In My Head** on the right side.*

Remember: because you are interpreting meaning—called inferencing—as well as your thoughts and feelings, there is no exact answer. While it is possible to misinterpret a message, anyone's thoughts and feelings are valid, no matter how they differ.

As the parent, you will have your own passage to copy on the following two pages. It is another passage from Kidd's book, as narrated by one of the protagonists, Hetty. You will also find a blank **On the Page/ In My Head** for your use in Appendix A.

The Invention of Wings **by Sue Monk Kidd**

Character: Hetty

Missus showed up and told Aunt-Sister to peel off my nasty coat and wash my face, then she said, "Hetty, this is Sarah's eleventh birthday and we are having a party for her."

She took a lavender ribbon from the top of the pie safe and circled it round my neck, tying a bow while Aunt-Sister peeled the black off my cheeks with her rag. Missus wound more ribbon round my waist. When I tugged, she told me in a sharp way, "Stop that fidgeting, Hetty! Be still."

Missus had done the ribbon too snug at my throat. It felt like I couldn't swallow. I searched for Aunt-Sister's eyes, but they were glued on the food trays. I wanted to tell her, *Get me free of this, help me, I need the privy.* I always had something smart to say, but my voice had run down my throat like a kitchen mouse.

I danced on one leg and the other. I thought what mauma had told me, "You be good coming up on Christmas cause that when they sell off the extra children or else send them to the fields." I didn't know one slave master Grimké had sold, but I knew plenty he'd sent to his plantation in the back country. That's where mauma had come from, bearing me inside her and leaving my daddy behind.

I stopped all my fidget then. My whole self went down in the hole where my voice was. I tried to do what they said God wanted. Obey, be quiet, be still.

Note: You will find a blank journal page for this lesson in Appendix A.

Children's Appreciation for Deep Meaning and Comprehension

The ability to comprehend text is a seemingly obvious ingredient in fluent writing, yet we often ask children to write about text, especially in copywork, without first engaging their thoughts and ensuring their full comprehension.

Because the primary goal of Intentional Copywork is to coordinate all the skills needed for fluent and effortless writing, it makes sense to begin with the most important one. Therefore, the first ingredient in this process is comprehension. We can write a short phrase that we don't understand by holding words in memory, but to fluently write an entire sentence of 10 words or more, we need to rely on meaning.

We have all experienced reading aloud to our children, only to suddenly realize we have no idea what we just read. We can engage automatically while reading without giving attention to meaning. When this happens, we are only *decoding*, since true reading requires comprehension. We can also copy words letter by letter, or copy sentences word by word, without engaging with meaning. This is not the goal.

Intentional Copywork is a meaningful writing tool because children give full attention to content, taking time to *read and comprehend* each passage. I like the strategy of On the Page (literal words in the passage) and In My Head (the inferred meaning of the passage) as a way to help children recognize and capture their own thoughts while reading. I discovered this exercise through my professional grapevine. Over the years, I expanded this approach, as we will explore throughout this book.

But first, let's return to Nemo, the chickadee feeder and writer, shown here with his sister Sigourney.

Nemo and Sigourney each had their own struggles with reading and writing: each with a unique set of strengths and challenges that influenced their homeschool day, every day.

Laurie's Journal

Nemo has the ability to take his intense interests and expand and build his ideas. He is a very strong personality, actually charismatic in many ways. His limit is language. He is a reluctant reader—it is not that he can't read, he just doesn't and can't articulate why. Nemo can comprehend during read-alouds, but he struggles to independently connect with reading.

Using variations of the On the Page/ In My Head strategies facilitated a turning point for Nemo. At age 10, Nemo could repeat ideas he read verbatim, but he had trouble translating what he read into his own words in order to engage in verbal conversations about meaning. Nemo had many great ideas, but he tended to disregard his thoughts as obvious and not worth mentioning.

Nemo began to record his ideas as he read. We started this notation informally, using his favorite genre and topic: nonfiction articles about animals. His mom would cut and paste the text into a document, then increase the margin on the right side, leaving a nice space for Nemo to write his thoughts as he read.

We encouraged Nemo to verbalize and then write his opinions:

✳ I like this

✳ This is true

✳ I know more about this fact

Nemo naturally added questions, which is often easier for children.

But teaching Nemo how to comment with deeper analysis was, as expected, more difficult.

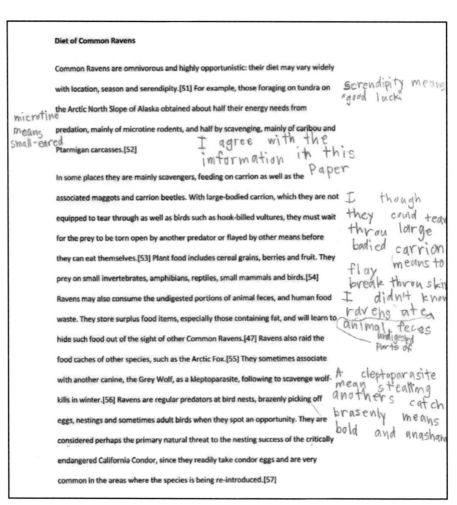

Diet of Common Ravens

Common Ravens are omnivorous and highly opportunistic: their diet may vary widely with location, season and serendipity.[51] For example, those foraging on tundra on the Arctic North Slope of Alaska obtained about half their energy needs from predation, mainly of microtine rodents, and half by scavenging, mainly of caribou and Ptarmigan carcasses.[52]

In some places they are mainly scavengers, feeding on carrion as well as the associated maggots and carrion beetles. With large-bodied carrion, which they are not equipped to tear through as well as birds such as hook-billed vultures, they must wait for the prey to be torn open by another predator or flayed by other means before they can eat themselves.[53] Plant food includes cereal grains, berries and fruit. They prey on small invertebrates, amphibians, reptiles, small mammals and birds.[54] Ravens may also consume the undigested portions of animal feces, and human food waste. They store surplus food items, especially those containing fat, and will learn to hide such food out of the sight of other Common Ravens.[47] Ravens also raid the food caches of other species, such as the Arctic Fox.[55] They sometimes associate with another canine, the Grey Wolf, as a kleptoparasite, following to scavenge wolf-kills in winter.[56] Ravens are regular predators at bird nests, brazenly picking off eggs, nestings and sometimes adult birds when they spot an opportunity. They are considered perhaps the primary natural threat to the nesting success of the critically endangered California Condor, since they readily take condor eggs and are very common in the areas where the species is being re-introduced.[57]

Handwritten annotations:

microtine means small-eared

Serendipity means "good luck"

I agree with the imformation in this Paper

I though they could tear throu large bodied carrion

flay means to break throu skin

I didn't know ravens ate animal feces undigested parts of

A cleptoparasite mean stealing anothers catch

brasenly means bold and unashamed

Nemo's first attempts to connect with text by writing opinions.

I use three strategies with Nemo and other children:

- ✸ **Writing together:** Nemo and I engaged in partnership writing, with each of us taking turns writing our thoughts about alternating paragraphs in a passage.

- ✸ **Modeling:** Nemo shared articles he had taken notes on, and I shared articles with my annotations for Nemo to read. We discussed each other's articles and commented on each other's comments.

- ✸ **Piggyback writing:** I discussed Nemo's written thoughts, using his ideas to inspire me to add more comments and vice versa. By showing Nemo how I elaborate on his ideas and encouraging him to elaborate on my ideas, we create a shared written conversation.

Each of these strategies helped Nemo discuss and write more thoughts over time, and eventually, Nemo became more comfortable capturing and sharing his ideas while reading.

Laurie's Journal

This approach supersedes the task mentality that busy, homeschooling parents so easily fall victim to, and replaces it with the higher intent of enriching the worldview of our children.

Our fleeting thoughts are ephemeral treasures that we must learn to grab out of habit. They allow us to bump right into the authentic voice we need for writing—the voice we are so often searching for. It is the right brain crying out before the left brain has a chance to leave our creativity threadbare.

Connecting Language to Language Arts ✻ Bits and Pieces

All of the lessons in this book encourage writing in **Bits and Pieces**: for yourself and hopefully for your children.

So what are Bits and Pieces? When we engage in writing our thoughts using smaller phrases and sentences, I call this writing Bits and Pieces. Bits and Pieces writing encourages kids to write because it's *not* complete paragraphs or papers. Children who fear writing, or struggle with reading and writing, are better able to engage in Bits and Pieces.

Seeing their ideas written on paper helps children validate their private internal conversations with text. In My Head activities, written in Bits and Pieces, help readers to identify their thoughts as "worthy" of further discussion—in both conversation and in additional writing.

In her book, *You Just Don't Understand*, Deborah Tannen suggests that males in particular tend to disregard fleeting thoughts as not worth sharing. I find that helping all children capture their fleeting thoughts is key to engaging in not only deep comprehension, but also original writing.

The level of simplicity or challenge may depend on the literature you select. It may depend on the activity. Or it may depend on each child's particular strengths and interests. Learning to capture thoughts and dig deep into understanding literature, both fiction and nonfiction, is not a simple skill. It is a skill that takes years to develop and master, as young minds grow in abstract thinking and life experience. Like us, our children achieve mastery in Bits and Pieces.

Bits and Pieces lessons are a means to explore deep meaning and comprehension within ourselves. The more we learn, the more we naturally share with our children. Each chapter sneaks Bits and Pieces of writing into your day, as a way of strengthening expressive writing. Modify and repeat the lessons throughout the year and for years to come. Engage in deep comprehension and writing in your own life—and for a lifetime.

Many children who struggle with writing—and let's face it, we all struggle with writing on some level—will appreciate using Bits and Pieces to help them explore their skills in stages.

Remember: learning one Tree well teaches us about the entire Forest of writing.

—Rita

"Most readers value annotations precisely because they are a private exchange between themselves and whatever book they happen to be talking back to."

—Mark O'Connell

Second Tree

Synergy: Finding the Real Story

Using picture books is another way to teach adults and children how to capture thoughts In My Head. Picture books are familiar, welcoming, and fun for our children and ourselves. For some children these books can help remove tension—their sense of being overwhelmed by text. Many picture books make perfect springboards for a deeper level of response. It is ironic that removing competing words can actually inspire a greater connection to text. The use of wordless (or nearly wordless) books demands that ideas and language concepts happen In My Head, since there are limited words On the Page.

Our awareness is heightened when reading picture books because quality illustrations conjure internal dialogue. Responding to pictures furthers our ability to notice and record our thoughts.

In My Head/On the Page ✺ *This Is Not My Hat* by Jon Klassen

The children's picture book *This Is Not My Hat* by Jon Klassen is an excellent choice for this exercise because it appeals to all ages—preschool through adulthood. The illustrations tell a different story than the narration, so reader interpretation becomes necessary to telling Klassen's story. *This Is Not My Hat* brilliantly plays between illustration and narration to force reader interaction and response. In fact, there simply is no story unless the reader responds.

Although *This Is Not My Hat* is a children's book, the ability to recognize an unreliable narrator is an advanced reading skill. I find most children only begin to recognize unreliable narrators around high school, or possibly middle school. In general, the time our children begin to judge our parenting skills is about the time they begin to judge other voices in their world, including a narrator's voice. Therefore, don't be afraid to use this exercise with tweens and teens.

Even though younger children may not be able to identify the story's discrepancies, they will enjoy capturing their thoughts as they read. The pictures are funny and the mood is intense, so young children will have plenty of reasons to think aloud as they turn each page.

For the deepest appreciation while exploring **In My Head/On the Page** for yourself, follow these steps carefully:

1. Do not open *This Is Not My Hat* before beginning this exercise because you will want to capture your first thoughts as each page reveals the story. Before you begin **In My Head/On the Page**, gather Post-its and a writing implement.

2. Your goal is to write your comments onto Post-it Notes, thereby creating a reverse writing activity: capturing what is **In My Head** and placing it **On the Page**. Don't skip a single page without recording your thoughts!

3. Find a quiet space to explore **In My Head/On the Page** apart from your children. You may later want to share this experience with each of your children, so it's best if you give yourself time to discover how **In My Head** thoughts contribute to the story.

4. Open to the first page of the story.

   The story begins with a little fish wearing a little hat. The narration reads: "This hat is not mine. I just stole it." Quite an opening hook, isn't it? Try to capture your initial thought, and write it on a Post-it. It does not have to be an entire sentence, but try to write more than one word. For instance, you may think: *thief!* But try to write the thought in a phrase: *a little thief!*

Typical **In My Head** reactions from my students include:

- "That's terrible!"
- "He's a thief"
- "Bad idea"
- "Not nice"

5. As you view each illustration and its text, continue to write your **In My Head** thoughts onto a new Post-it Note, placing it **On the Page** for each image throughout the book. Enjoy both the story and the illustrations.

6. Once you have completed *This Is Not My Hat*, and all your Post-it Notes are on each spread, return to the beginning of the book. This time, notice the symbiotic relationship between each narration (by the little fish), each illustration, and then each Post-it Note with your **In My Head** thought. As you progress, you will begin to appreciate that Klassen's story is not a story unless you—the reader—react.

Connecting Art to Language Arts ✖ *This Is Not My Hat*

In the best picture books, the words have a story to tell, the pictures have a story to tell, and the two together are greater than the sum of the parts. *This Is Not My Hat* by Jon Klassen is a great example of this synergy.

What fascinates me most about Klassen's illustrations is the simplicity. In our busy lives we have all learned that, ironically, it takes a concerted effort to keep things simple. This is true in art as well as writing. I am reminded of Mark Twain's famous comment that if he'd had more time, he would have written a shorter letter.

Take a moment to appreciate Klassen's frugal illustrations in *This Is Not My Hat*. In the second, third, fourth, and fifth spreads of the book, he presents the same big fish in the same position in the same simplified background. The only thing that changes is the fish's eye. And yet Klassen manages to convey a wealth of emotions, easily interpreted by the reader. His illustrations move the story forward with the very repetitiveness of the scene, causing the reader to want to turn the page—much like a good writer can convey so much in so few words…if they have the time!

—*Tracy*

We now appreciate how In My Head contributes to what is written On the Page. Without our response, there really is no story at all! *This Is Not My Hat* serves as a metaphor demonstrating that, in order for story to be story, synergy is required between the reader and the writer.

In our first two trees, we explore the question: Is reading truly reading without interpretation, response, and internal conversation with the writer?

This question brings to mind the age-old riddle: If a tree falls in the forest and nobody hears it, is there sound? Just as sound isn't quite sound without a listener, reading isn't quite reading without an interpreter.

Connecting Language to Language Arts ✸ Abstract Thinking

As an adult reading *This Is Not My Hat* by Jon Klassen, I am immediately aware of the dichotomy between the text (the words On the Page) and the pictures (which evoke In My Head interpretation). I discover contradiction at the start of the book when the little fish-thief says, "And he probably won't wake up for a long time," as I simultaneously view a menacing-looking fish with eyes wide open. I understand that narrators may be unreliable.

Because the text does not match the pictures, two separate stories take place concurrently. Our ability to perceive these two plotlines is a higher-level thinking skill that is both social and literary.

Socially, we judge when a person (or character) is in error, as well as the typical human reasons for error: poor judgment, deceit, ignorance, or denial. The fish-thief may be motivated by any of these. We draw on social reasoning for In My Head interpretation.

Young children typically do not understand the concept of an unreliable narrator; my students do not judge the little fish as "wrong" (unreliable) until the illustrations join the narration at the end of the book. Without fail, one page triggers young children's social thinking: when the fish-thief states, "There is someone who saw me already/ But he said he wouldn't tell anyone which way I went." My younger students know the crab will tell. When I inquire into their insight, students reveal their general knowledge that *someone will always tell*. Students also root for the big fish, wanting justice for the crime, and are satisfied with the ending.

From a literary perspective, requiring maturity and abstract reasoning, we understand that a first-person narrator only tells a story from one perspective. Pictures, however, provide a third person perspective in this story: the reader is observing the large fish, and can guess what he is thinking. We have the literary thinking skills—flexible thinking skills—to tell a reader's version of the real story. Older children and adults understand that Klassen's little fish thief is an *unreliable narrator,* that a conflict is underway, that a climax is coming, and that the problem will be resolved. We worry for the little fish, even while feeling annoyance at his justification for stealing.

(continued)

Connecting Language to Language Arts ✸ Abstract Thinking

(continued)

In the words of a 13-year-old student, *This Is Not My Hat* "Looks like a children's book—but it's not!" Because young children are not mature abstract thinkers, Klassen's book is a way for us to gain insight into the level of our children's In My Head thinking. In My Head/On the Page provides an opportunity to show children how their thoughts are a part of a story.

Remember: without the reader's In My Head response, there is no story!

—*Rita*

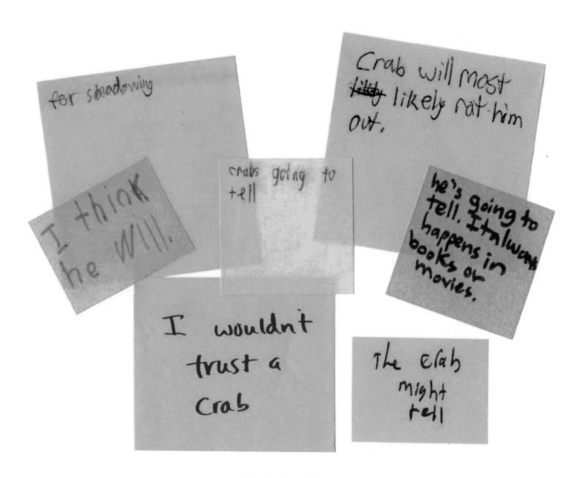

Crab Will Tell.

How to Teach the Lesson to Your Children

Have each of your children pick a color of Post-it Notes and pen or pencil, and engage in this lesson individually.

> *Artists use illustrations to help us imagine in our heads not only what is happening in a story, but what the characters are feeling and thinking. The illustrations demonstrate the mood in the story as well as the action. This mood helps us to imagine and inspires thoughts.*
>
> *Today you are going to look at a picture book with few words. Your job is to react "out loud" every time we turn the page.*
>
> *Once you react out loud, you will capture your own words by writing them on a Post-it Note and sticking it **On the Page**. In this way, each of your reactions adds to your own interpretation of the story—your own **In My Head** thinking. Once you write your words on the Post-it Note, you will place your notes **On the Page**.*
>
> *If you remember, we called the words that are **In My Head** "inferential thinking" because they are based on what we think, rather than on what is written **On the Page**. In this book, little is written, so everything we write on our Post-it Notes is what we think or feel.*
>
> *Each of us will have different responses in this reverse exercise called **In My Head/On the Page**. Once you put all your Post-it Notes on the book's pages, we will start over. We will look back through the book together and read all the Post-it Notes. Reading each other's words might inspire more thoughts. If you have new thoughts, you can write them down and put any new notes on the page as we "re-read" the book together.*
>
> *Remember: because you are inferencing (interpreting meaning) as well as recording your thoughts and feelings, there is no exact answer. Everyone's thoughts and feelings are valid, no matter how they differ.*

If you prefer, after each of your children has completed this exercise, you can have all of your family members view the book together. Everyone can place their Post-its on each page as you all read the book, in order to facilitate further discussion. [See Crab Will Tell illustration.]

You can also try this exercise using the book *Blart—A Little Blob of Art* by Tracy Molitors, a book we will use again in the Sixth Tree activity.

Important Modifications to Consider:

Work to a level of success, not frustration. Use your best judgment for each child, and don't be afraid to modify the lesson.

* Due to the amount of writing, young children may be unable to write as they react. You can act as a recorder, writing down their words as they exclaim and letting them place their Post-it Note **On the Page**.

* You can record your children's responses and then encourage them to copy **In My Head** thoughts onto Post-it Notes and put them in the book. Remember to number each verbal reaction to correspond with each page.

* Some children may need you to share the work of handwriting. Take turns writing for your struggling writers. Help them by *Partnership Writing* either every other Post-it Note or any difficult spelling words expressed in their thoughts.

Laurie's Journal

In my house, because of competitive personalities, the goal is to get to the point where my kids would enjoy sharing ideas without thinking another idea is a negation of their own.

"Books can truly change our lives: the lives of those who read them, and the lives of those who write them. Readers and writers alike discover things they never knew about the world and about themselves."

—from *Time Cat* by Lloyd Alexander

Third Tree

Connecting with Characters

I remember crying over Charlotte's death when I read *Charlotte's Web*. Charlotte created a turning point for me and my relationship with text. It was the first time I can recall missing a character's place in my life. I felt that, like Wilber, I had lost a friend in Charlotte. While reading the book, I daydreamed I was Fern in an effort to extend the story in my mind. *Charlotte's Web* was THE BOOK that turned me into "a reader": one who lives life constantly craving engagement with text.

How about you? What was THE BOOK that changed the way you see character? Or, if you cannot recall THE BOOK, perhaps you have a few that stand out as influential.

Here is my list:

★ *Charlotte's Web*

★ *Little House on the Prairie*

★ *To Kill a Mockingbird*

Write your list in your journal or on the page provided here and in Appendix A. On the left side, include at least three influential books. These books do not have to be impressive by anyone else's standards; they only had to impress you.

Now, think about what you discovered about yourself as a reader when you read those books, and write your thoughts on the right side.

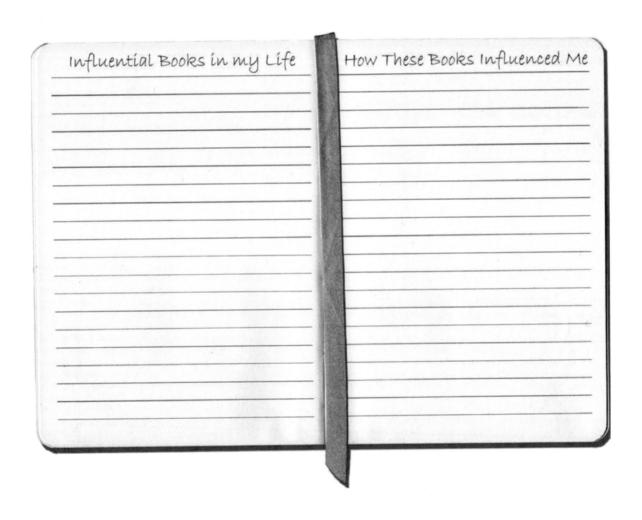

Influential Books in my Life | How These Books Influenced Me

Here are mine:

★ *Charlotte's Web* – I developed an emotional response to characters that deepened my relationship with stories.

★ *Little House on the Prairie* – I developed a habit of reading every day as I moved from one book in the series to another, so from that time forward, I always had to have a book in my life. I transitioned from "I don't know what to read" to "I will find what to read."

★ *To Kill a Mockingbird* – This was the first novel that made me aware of the expertise of the author and my own skills (or lack thereof) as a writer. Although I may have read other well-written books before *To Kill a Mockingbird*, I clearly remember thinking, "This is the gold standard for writing." Harper Lee was the first writer I tried to imitate. I share this story with my students when they read *To Kill a Mockingbird*, hoping they will connect with Lee's writing as well.

Tracy's Journal

As I read Rita's comments on influential books, I realized that I grew up with a slightly different experience. Books have always been significant and important in my life, but I was an indifferent reader until early high school. My mother was talented and generous in her read-aloud efforts with our family. Consequently, the books that changed my life, and eventually turned me into the avid reader that I am today, were all read aloud to me.

The greatest change in the way I perceived story occurred the summer that I turned nine when Mom read the Lord of the Rings *trilogy aloud to our family. Prior to that experience, I was not actively aware that a book had the ability to transport me to another place and time entirely— that imaginative settings could hijack my mind long after the reading was done—that fictional characters could make me weep with joy or sorrow. The list goes on and includes other books like* The Incredible Journey *and* A Wrinkle in Time, *both of which refined my understanding of story and writing as a craft.*

I think that I needed to reach an age when I could emulate my mother's theatrical reading skills before I could truly enjoy reading a novel by myself. I lacked the ability to connect to the text, and Mom served as my bridge until I was able to do it on my own and In My Head.

Rita's Journal

I challenge kids to discover THE BOOK for themselves—the story that changes the way they think about reading. Back in the day, when I had fewer students, I used to tell my students who disliked reading that when they discovered their book—THE BOOK—that changed their relationship with reading, I would read it as well. One young teen took my challenge to heart, and after her months' vacation, brought me the entire Twilight *series, dropping them on my desk with a heavy thump.*

"Here they are," she said. "I found the book—books! —that is THE BOOK! You promised you'd read it when I found it, and I can't wait to talk about them!"

How could I resist such enthusiasm? So I read the Twilight *series, joining her in the national teen-girl character-connection debate (of the romantic nature): Team Jacob vs. Team Edward. She debated with me in writing, so that was my reward.*

For years I kept my IF YOU LOVE IT, I WILL READ IT promise with my students. Consequently, I have read quite a few books, even some I would not have chosen: the inane— Captain Underpants; *kid spy books—*Alex Rider; *teen romances—*Twilight; *horror—*Odd Thomas; *sports—quite a few by Chris Crutcher; fantasy—*Percy Jackson; *and sci-fi—*Ender's Game. *Sometimes it is a stretch, but sometimes a perfect character bond is formed.*

The shared reading experience is ongoing with my own children, who are no longer children. My family promise: I will read some of your favorite books and join in a book discussion. I am lucky that my family will reciprocate.

Now, let's explore character together—you and I, then you and your children…

Drawing Is Seeing ✳ Cartooning Characters

One day Tracy shared this idea: those who write should draw, and those who draw should write. According to Tracy, because drawing focuses our thoughts, it brings an image more clearly into our minds. This focus brings insight to writing as well. The artist's adage that **Drawing Is Seeing** can help us clarify our thoughts in writing.

I avoid all forms of drawing because it is not in my skill set, yet I began to see how illustration can add insight to my writing, and in writing with children. I began to see how drawing helps to illustrate concepts. In accepting her own challenge, Tracy began writing stories around her art, resulting in greater intensity and mood.

When I view drawing as a skill, I feel inadequate, and I don't do it. But when I view drawing as a tool, I realize its value, so I am willing to try. Because many students are as bashful about drawing as I am, I sometimes use clip art as a means of illustration. But Tracy has convinced me that even my lowly stick figures have value in generating more words In My Head. So we all have Tracy to thank for this exercise!

We are using cartooning to create a character connection—first together, and then with our children. Let's select a few more passages from the novel *The Invention of Wings* by Sue Monk Kidd. Because I am a *word* person, I tend to relate to thoughts and feelings in characters, rather than trying to picture them In My Head. But when I begin to draw, I have to collect my thoughts and feelings and bring them together in one place. Writing Bits and Pieces around my cartoon deepens my image of the character, enriching my understanding.

My son is currently in a drawing class about line. As he explained to me, he is learning to see line as it actually exists, not just his idea of how line *should* look. Understanding—or truly seeing—gives the proper perspective. In this same way, drawing causes me to examine the *outlines* of a character, not as I normally see life, but in a way that gives a new perspective.

New perspective equals perception. Looking at characters from a relational perspective deepens our insight or "In My Head-sight."

Connecting Art to Language Arts ✸ What's Special?

Sketch artists learn quickly that **Drawing Is Seeing.** As soon as I make an effort to reproduce something on paper, I am forced to study it in a way that casual observation does not require. I must now observe fine details. Everything becomes relevant. How does the length of a forearm compare to the upper arm? How does a shadow cut across the surface of a flower?

This level of detail can scare off some people, but it doesn't need to—even stick figures can benefit from seeing more carefully. When my children were young and wanted to draw an animal or make one from clay, we would always play the **What's Special** game. If they wanted a horse, I would ask them to picture a horse and then tell me, "What's Special about a horse?" They might answer, "It has a mane!" "Good one!" I might say. "What else?" With prompting they would point out that it has a long tail and a fairly long neck—or that it has four long, skinny legs compared to its body. And then they would draw a stick figure horse. As long as they added the details they saw, everyone knew it was a horse, and therefore, it was an insightful drawing.

Drawing Is Seeing.

—*Tracy*

Here is Tracy's sketch of the character of Williams from the book *The Invention of Wings*.

Tracy's drawing is based on her prior knowledge of how a wealthy young man in the 1800s might look. Based on the passage, Tracy drew him looking confident and comfortable in formal society.

Experiment with drawing one of your favorite characters. Ask yourself **What's Special** about this character. How can you distinguish your character from the basic hangman? Sometimes the physical act of drawing can become the intellectual bridge to span the gap from reading to analysis, from simple decoding to deeper thinking.

Tracy's Journal: *Drawing Williams*

Williams was an interesting choice for a character drawing because he is not "'well-drawn" in the story. He is a minor character, so frankly, I didn't remember much about him other than what was in the passage. When I first attempted a sketch of Williams, I saw him as a gawky, awkward young man.

But a funny thing happened on the way to my drawing. I was asking myself questions about Williams and rereading the passage, and I began to remember his larger role in the story. I realized that I did not really see him as awkward—young, yes, but handsome and assured, with motives that aren't obvious. He was interested in Sarah because she was different, rich and vulnerable, and he had already developed some cynicism toward his society. As I drew this young man, I started to think of Snidely Whiplash, and so I added the mustache and the slightly villainous eyebrows. These were fairly sophisticated concepts, so I doubt if my drawing reveals all that, but the point is that it happened In My Head because I was attempting to draw him.

Now it is your turn:

Read and select one of the three passages provided on the following pages or from a favorite book. Then draw an illustration of what you imagine about the character, adding Bits and Pieces of writing to capture In My Head thoughts. Deeper understanding is reflected when we write ideas in our own words. Think of captioning the cartoon as capturing new thoughts.

Bring yourself to the drawing with whatever skill level you possess. This is not an exercise in creating a masterpiece: it is an exercise in connecting with the character on a deeper level. Think of the drawing as an expression of your thoughts and emotion: an exploration or imaginative play.

You can place your illustration with the passage or on another piece of paper.

Connecting Art to Language Arts ✗ Drawing Is Seeing

During a discussion about drawing characters, I found myself playing the **What's Special** game with Rita. After assurances that stick figures would work great, and that she could draw in Bits and Pieces on a Post-it Note, I convinced her to try for herself. She chose Scout from *To Kill a Mockingbird* because she is a character who is wonderfully developed and familiar to many of us.

She started with the basic figure, but being Rita, she began embellishing the Scout image with distinctive details—without much prompting. Rita also began writing her comments on the drawing, naturally moving the exercise back toward writing (in Bits and Pieces). The exercise was a clear example of why **Drawing Is Seeing**—even at a stick figure level.

Rita's Scout Drawing.

Cartooning is often commentary. Many of Rita's ideas could be used in writing about this character, but she might not have generated such a rich character illustration in writing without first exploring the actual illustration in drawing. For children who struggle with writing, drawing can help to inspire them to dig deeper into character.

—*Tracy*

The Invention of Wings by Sue Monk Kidd

Character: Sarah

Setting: Charleston, February, 1811

Sitting before the mirror in my room, I stared at my face while Handful and six-year-old Nina wove my ponytail into braids with the aim of looping them into a circlet at the nape of my neck. Earlier I'd rubbed my face with salt and lemon-vinegar, which was Mother's formula for removing ink spots. It had lightened my freckles, but not erased them, and I reached for the powder muff to finish them off...

I'd entered society two years ago, at sixteen, thrust into the lavish round of balls, teas, musical salons, horseraces, and picnics, which, according to Mother, meant the dazzling doors of Charleston had flung open and female life could begin in earnest. In other words, I could take up the business of procuring a husband. How highborn and moneyed this husband turned out to be would depend entirely on the allure of my face, the delicacy of my physique, the skill of my seamstress, and the charisma of my tête-à-tête. Notwithstanding my seamstress, I arrived at the glittery entrance like a lamb to slaughter.

The Invention of Wings by Sue Monk Kidd

Character: Sarah, describing Hetty (also known as Handful)

At seventeen, [Handful] was a prodigy with the needle, even more so than her mother. She now sewed most of my attire.

As Handful stretched up on tiptoe to retrieve the dress, I noticed how undeveloped she was—her body lithe and skinny as a boy's. She didn't reach five feet and never would. But as small as she was, it was still her eyes that drew attention. I'd once heard a friend of Thomas' refer to her as the pretty, yellow-eyed Negress. . .

As she passed the fireplace with the dress in her arms, I noticed the frown that seemed permanently etched in her features, as if by narrowing her enormous eyes she felt less of the world could reach her. It seemed she'd begun to feel the boundaries of her life more keenly, that she'd arrived at some moment of reckoning. The past week, Mother had denied her a pass to the market for some minor, forgettable reason, and she'd taken it hard . . . I'd said, "I'm sorry, Handful, I know how you must feel."

It seemed to me I *did* know what it felt to have one's liberty curtailed, but she blazed up at me. "So we just the same, me and you? That's why you the one to shit in the pot and I'm the one to empty it?"

The Invention of Wings by Sue Monk Kidd

Character: Burke Williams, in conversation with Sarah

"Are you visiting here?" I asked.

"Not at all, my family's home is on Vanderhorst. But I can read your thoughts. You're trying to place my family. *Williams, Williams, wherefore art thou Williams?*" He laughed. "If you're like the others, you're worried I'm an artisan or a laborer, or worse, an *aspirer*."

I caught my breath. "Oh, I didn't mean—I'm not concerned with that sort of thing."

"It's all in jest—I can see you're not like the others. Unless, of course, you're off-put to learn my family runs the silversmith shop on Queen Street. I'll inherit it one day."

…"I see I've offended you," he said. "I intended to be charming, but I've been mocking instead. It's because my station is an awkward topic for me. I'm ill at ease with it."

I turned back to him, astonished that he'd been so free with his thoughts. I hadn't known a young man to display this kind of vulnerability.

Drawing Is Seeing ✸ Cartooning Characters with Your Children

Now it's time to encourage your children to connect with character.

Think about your children and how they like to draw. They may like to assemble clip art. They may prefer to use paint, crayons, markers or traditional drawing pencils. They may favor paper art, using torn pieces of colored and textured papers.

Consult them regarding what medium will be most inspirational. As we have illustrated, a simple pencil and Post-it will suffice.

Help your children choose a character from a book they are currently reading or use the passages provided in Appendix B.

How to Teach this Lesson to Your Children

One of the ways we can appreciate reading and writing is to think about the characters in a story and see them in a new way.

Today we are going to cartoon one of the characters from your book using clues from the text as well as any other things you know about the character from reading the story.

Read your passage two times. Let's underline any phrases that give us clues about the character and what we can draw. The clues can relate to how the character looks, such as clothes, hair color, or height. But there may be other clues that are not as obvious. For instance, there may be clues about the character's facial expressions. There may be clues about attitude. There may be clues about where the character likes to be or what she likes to say. There may be clues about the character's problems. Use all of these clues to draw your character.

If you remember, we called the words that are **In My Head** *inferential thinking because they are based on what we think in response to what is written* **On the Page***. Try to use your* **In My Head** *thinking to help you create* **Bits and Pieces** *of writing about your character. This writing helps to put captions on your cartoon.*

Now think about the character's problem in the story. Is there something you can draw to represent the character's problem? Or you could have the character hold an item that represents a problem or desire.

You could give your character a sign to carry. What would it say?

For example, in the story This Is Not My Hat, *the hat would represent the fish's problem or conflict (stealing from a bigger fish), and the tall plants might represent his desire to hide from the consequences of stealing.*

Remember: because you are interpreting meaning—what we call inferencing—as well as your thoughts and feelings, there is no exact answer. Everyone's drawings are equally valid, and we can learn a lot by seeing different approaches to drawing character—making this exercise a rich source of conversation. The goal is to get to know your character better by drawing as many **In My Head** *ideas as you can.*

Connecting Language to Language Arts ✸ Handwriting

It is interesting to note that most of my students who struggle with pencil grasp and handwriting enjoy drawing. They can easily wield a crayon, pencil, marker, or paint brush as long as they are not writing letters. Recent research into the area of *dysgraphia* reveals that the difficulty in handwriting is related to weakness in sound-to-letter connection, not fine motor control. Handwriting requires access to areas of the language system needed to read, not areas accessed for fine movement. In working with children who avoid handwriting, I begin by showing them that they have the fine motor skills to write. Strengthening sound-to-letter connection, rather than pencil grasp, helps children with dysgraphia succeed in handwriting. For these children, Cartooning might be a relief: writing in Bits and Pieces is certainly less stressful than writing an entire passage.

By contrast, children who are art challenged, like me, may groan in protest. Showing your children my humble illustrations may encourage them to give cartooning a go.

—Rita

Character	Sketch	Rank	Likes
Scipio		Leader 1	likes to have everything perfect
Prosper		on the edge of the group	Likes Bo
Bo		Follower, but can break rules	swepts likes to steal like Scipio
Hornet		Unspoken Leader 2	books

Nemo's character study from *Thief Lord* by Cornelia Funke.

DOC ♡

Doc is very special to me because he is so sweet and gentle, he has a beautiful colour, he can go fast, and he is very handsome. He has a star, stripe, and snip and he has half a cornet on his back right leg. Doc is the leader of all of the horses at Woodside. He is even the leader of Brody. Doc loves me and I love him. His favourite place to be brushed is under the mane. When I brush under Doc's mane he loves it and he wiggles his lips with delight. I look forward to every time I ride Doc. I love the red colour of Doc with his red blanket and the colour of the red lead rope Chloe bought for him. I can't wait to gallop Doc. He is a very fun horse to ride. I have enjoyed Doc ever since I got him.

Sigourney's understanding of character influences her original writing.

On the Floor and On the Stage

THE BOOK for Sigourney and Nemo was *Redwall* by Brian Jacques.

Because of their children's intense love for animals, Laurie and her husband had tried introducing this series to Sigourney and Nemo in the past, but they were not interested in "animals that were not real."

Laurie and I began a journey to help Nemo and Sigourney connect with story characters on a more personal level—helping them to appreciate characters' personalities and, in the case of *Redwall*, their voices and humor.

Once Laurie and I encouraged Nemo and Sigourney to connect with the characters, *Redwall* sparked the children's interest in writing their own stories. Both children began to imitate Jacques's writing. They used their love for facts in their fiction to create plausible stories—much the way professional writers use facts to give their stories authenticity.

Sigourney struggled with pretend in all areas of her learning, so story comprehension and creative writing were difficult as well. She did not engage in pretend play with her toys, nor did she create dialogue in play. Sigourney, like many children, is drawn to structure and building. Grammar was fun; creative writing was not. Concrete ideas were pleasing; abstract ideas were a stretch.

When Sigourney listened to stories, she focused on details, but often missed the key ideas needed to hold the story together. Therefore, she could not retell stories effectively, or engage in complex discussions around story. Sigourney needed to understand how to pretend, so the best way to explore her connection with books was through character.

Sigourney began engaging with story **On the Floor**. She began with the book *Frog and Toad* by Arnold Lobel. Laurie helped Sigourney copy pictures from the book, then create character puppets by taping the pictures onto sticks. The sticks were placed into slits in a shoe box, creating a mini theater. Sigourney then used her character puppets to retell narratives. The more she acted out the story, the better she comprehended the tale and its key elements.

On the Floor includes any pretend play inspired by stories. Sigourney began to lift lines from *Redwall* and borrow them in her play with her toy animals, helping her animals talk to each other. This soon led to pretend dialogue, and play acting with her toys gave Sigourney great ideas for writing. Sigourney needed time On the Floor in order to better connect, comprehend, and create. Discovering dialogue was key for her. Children's comprehension grows through play, so we encourage time and space for On the Floor exploration.

Sigourney's Journal

The badger said to himself, "I think I would like this nice warm house." The squirrels woke up.

The squirrels yelled, "There's a badger in our territory!" The squirrels tried clawing and hitting, but it didn't work. The badger hit back. Then, the squirrels all waved their tails around and their tails accidentally hit the badger in the head.

"I'll get you this time!" said one of the squirrels and he turned around and bit the badger. The badger ran away without saying anything.

The lonely badger came back that night and said to the squirrels, "May I live in this hole with you?"

Nemo easily created characters, but like all children, he struggled to help his reader comprehend his ideas. This ability to understand the reader's perspective is a lifelong pursuit, one I struggle with every time I write. Nemo learned to define his characters for his readers by first illustrating them for himself.

Here is a sample of Nemo's story character chart:

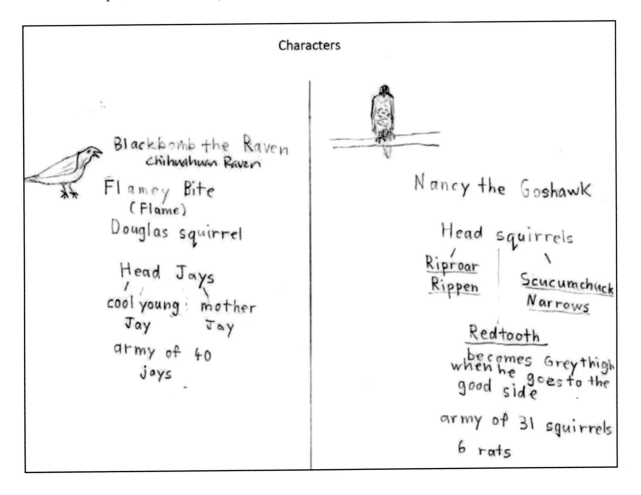

Helping children move characters off and on the page—from book to floor and floor to paper—is an excellent way to create character connections. Older children may do this by moving from book to stage, acting out scenes, dialogue, or extending a story into a satirical play or movie. Dress-up should be encouraged, no matter the age.

Here is Sigourney connecting with her character, the Snow Owl. She loves to dress up and create, so she often puts herself into her character's world through role play. Play helps Sigourney embellish her stories In My Head, so she can put them On the Page.

Sigourney's Journal

The Snowy Owl hung on the trap door and the trap door swung open quietly, with no creaking.

"Okay, I've got it open," Snowy Owl whispered.

Our own children constantly acted out stories and movies **On the Stage**, both in their play, and as a way of illustrating story for improved comprehension. They inspired each other in creating sock puppets to act out the basic story arc of *Uncle Tom's Cabin* by Harriet Beecher Stowe, as well as the battle at Fort Sumter.

Tracy's daughter Claire built an imposing cardboard puppet theater for her retelling of *Macbeth*, which she cleverly titled *MacBook*. By putting her handmade sock puppets onto cardboard tubes, she could easily manipulate multiple characters to retell her story in her Sock Puppet Theater.

My children still fondly recall the day I pulled out a large white board and illustrated the entire plotline of *Twelfth Night* by Shakespeare. I knew the story's convolutions (who loved whom, who was a male and who was a female, etc.) would be complicated, so I relied on my little stick figures to prepare them for the tale. They loved that lesson, helping me to realize the power of cartooning as commentary—about story and life.

It is important to foster children's connections with characters by encouraging their daydreams and imaginings. Children who identify with character are more likely to seek out future relationships through story. Connecting with character does not guarantee a love of reading, but it is a necessary ingredient.

Fourth Tree

Discovering the Writer

When we talk to people who see themselves as readers, one common experience they share is a love for the writer's words. No matter the genre, readers stop and appreciate writing, developing relationships with their favorite authors.

When we talk to people who see themselves as writers, one common experience they share is a love for their *own* words—not all their words, but enough to keep *writers* writing again and again.

As a child and teen, I created a poem or story, then read and reread it aloud to myself, chewing each savory morsel. Hearing my own voice, and watching my

thoughts unfold onto a page felt like discovering new territory—uncharted lands within my own mind—lands I had never seen before.

Noticing and collecting quotes from our own writing and the writing of others lays a path to our discovery of these new lands. Discussing books and reading favorite selections aloud to one another is a valuable ingredient to introduce in family book-talk. Making our own personal connection with the writer's words is a precursor to lively discussion—tilling the soil for our children's growth as lovers of literature.

Laurie's Journal

I crave literature and I make no time for it in my day, but I plan to schedule guilt-free time to commune with moments of beauty; otherwise, I fear I will unexpectedly find the color of my spirit slightly faded from malnourishment.

In his book *Everyone Can Write,* Peter Elbow explores ways to help his university students connect with literature. He cuts passages into fragments, distributing them to students to use as writing prompts. He has them borrow features from the text and use those features in their own creative works. Borrowing text, Elbow notes, "[leads] us to write pieces that say things we didn't know we were going to say—but that it turns out we seem to want to say."

Writers use Bits and Pieces of their ideas and then combine them into passages in an order that conveys their message to us. So what if we try this? Take Bits and Pieces of the writer's passage and combine them in our own way.

We might discover a new way of expressing ourselves, or we may just have fun. But playing with phrases On the Page, and combining them in new ways, helps us relate the writer's words to our own lives. We converse with a writer in much the same way we converse with friends—agreeing with ideas, repeating key thoughts, nodding along and even interrupting. Conversation encourages In My Head thinking, especially because we are expected to take our turn, not just to listen passively.

Connecting Art to Language Arts ✸ Laying a Path

Many times I have heard Rita talk about working to a level of success. She means that kids learn and grow through their accomplishments, not their failures. They need to stretch, but not so far that they become overwhelmed. Repeated failure only teaches children to believe that what they want is unattainable. With no path to guide them, children may lose their way and stumble without direction through the Forest. The very worst is if children give up, believing they can never become readers and writers.

Rita advises parents that they are creating a path for their children. Each new skill or successful activity is a new stone laid on that trail. **Laying a Path** helps our children move forward from where they are. By helping children lay each stone successfully, one skill at a time, we guide them down a path to literacy.

Not surprisingly, this same concept has helped in teaching art to both children and adults. I would not introduce an art course by asking a student to paint a copy of the Mona Lisa. Instead I might ask a student to look in a mirror and make a sad face. See what that face does to your eyes, eyebrows, and lips. Can you draw a basic sad face using simple lines in a simple circle? After this fundamental instruction, students now have some success in capturing emotion in a face. From there we can begin to move through a whole range of emotions: first simple ones—sad, happy, startled; then more complicated ones—belligerent, confused, sorry. We have begun Laying a Path to cartooning!

I introduce fine art concepts like watercolor painting with the same one-stone-at-a-time approach. While a lovely John Singer Sargent painting can provide inspiration, it would likely discourage new students from attempting a similar watercolor painting—it's a lot harder than it looks! Instead we do fun activities and Bits and Pieces of art that offer opportunities for confident self-expression and joy. Along that path we begin to lay more stones for brushstrokes, washes, color mixing, glazing, textures and a host of other techniques that will enrich our painting experience.

—*Tracy*

Creating Phrase Trees

As we journey through the Forest, we stop on our path for an activity called **Phrase Trees**. Phrase Trees encourage children to draw out interesting thoughts and phrases within a text, and apply those thoughts to their own lives. Phrase Trees grow from text—entwining the roots of literature with the roots of personal experience.

Phrase Trees are a fun activity to do with your children to help them connect with the writer. They combine each child's artistic expression with a deeper exploration of writing.

New standards in language arts demand that children recognize and analyze not only literary concepts, but also a writer's style: word choice, bias, voice, and other complex rhetorical devices. Children must uncover what is not readily visible—excavate and elaborate.

At the same time, *explicit* instruction in how to do this is falling out of vogue. Children are to learn through *discovery*, by *uncovering that which is hidden*. Discovery, or learning through experience, is seen as a means for creative problem solving, and is surely more fun than being spoon-fed answers.

Except *discovery* may fall into what I call The Easter Basket Debacle. I hid my children's baskets every Easter, playing "hot and cold" as they searched the house for their goodies. They had fun until I hid one basket *too well*. Not only did that child give up looking, but all my children felt annoyed. Delightful discovery turned to agitated floundering in a matter of moments!

The same principle can be applied to learning. We want delightful discovery, but we need to create a path. We need to ensure a fair level of success, so kids are encouraged to keep looking. We can't hide the answers too well without risking an Easter Basket Debacle. **Laying a Path** to discovery finds the balance between unearthing and feeling buried—it is not the antithesis of creative exploration.

Phrase Trees, a form of *Found Poetry*, create a path to help children successfully extract meaningful quotes within a passage. In Found Poetry, the poet pulls words and phrases from any source to create a poem. When creating Phrase Trees, your children select a collection of phrases from a literary passage they enjoy and artistically arrange those phrases to create an individual writing piece. Phrase Trees are a wonderful combination of poetry and graphic design.

When children design Phrase Trees, they connect with the writer's ideas on a more personal level and create their own interpretation. By focusing on phrases, children

✷   read closely and connect with text,

✷   judge which phrases are the most interesting, and

✷   create artistic self-expression.

Connecting Art to Language Arts   ✷   Graphic Expression

Graphic art has many purposes—to convey ideas quickly and clearly, to present information in a more readable fashion, to evoke feelings, or simply to make something more pleasing. To create a Phrase Tree, focus on the phrases you appreciate, deciding the best way to represent them graphically to bring out what you want to emphasize.

Color: Color conveys emotion, so choose color purposefully. For instance, orange can convey energy, playfulness, alarm, or excitement. Color can also provide associations with bigger concepts, such as green representing a forest or growth.

Shape: Many phrases include or evoke images, so the words can be formed into that item, such as a boat, whip, or waves. In addition, words can be configured into a common shape, like triangles, squares, or circles, to express mood, volume, or intensity.

Size: Size conveys importance or volume—the bigger, the louder, or the more the phrase matters to you. Size can also indicate advancing or receding thoughts.

Position: The phrase most important to you should become the central root of your Phrase Tree. Horizontal positions are likely to be noticed first. Likewise, since we read from left to right, the left side of the page is usually read first. Words located in the middle or at the top of the page can indicate a dominant thought.

—*Tracy*

Connecting Language to Language Arts ✷ Powerful Quotes

In schools across America children are required to find *powerful quotes* in text. They must then use these quotes as *supportive evidence* in writing assignments.

However, children need time and practice engaging with text in order to distinguish which phrases contain powerful thoughts. **Phrase Trees** help children to discover and uncover the *meaning of meaningful* text and to analyze powerful phrases. Thus, Phrase Trees teach kids what constitutes *supportive evidence* for their writing, making this opaque concept more clear. Phrase Trees are enjoyable to boot!

In addition, when children read their Phrase Trees aloud, they begin to insert the writer's words into their own spoken sentences—thereby practicing the grammatical flexibility needed for embedding quotes smoothly in their writing.

—Rita

Let's look at some samples of **Phrase Trees**:

Student Phrase Tree from *Little Women* by Louisa May Alcott.

Student Phrase Tree from *Their Eyes Were Watching God* by Zora Neale Hurston.

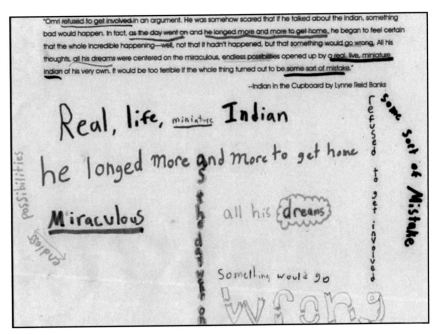

Student Phrase Tree from *The Indian in the Cupboard* by Lynne Reid Banks.

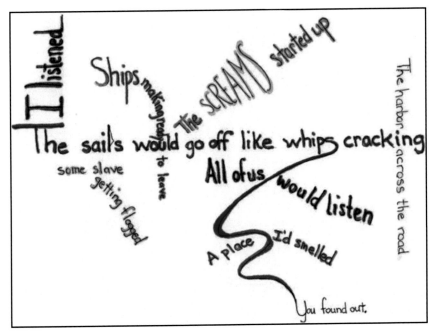

Tracy's Phrase Tree from *The Invention of Wings* by Sue Monk Kidd.

Laurie's Journal

The Phrase Tree exercise reminded me how much Nemo and Sigourney loved putting their original stories in a binder with plastic sleeves. They have sat and read their own words and reread their stories to each other so many times. They cherish when Rita highlights her favorite phrases within their writing. My children anticipate sharing their words and waiting for someone else to discover their importance. Celebrating Nemo's and Sigourney's original words is one of the most meaningful things we have done.

Reading is thinking and thinking needs expression.

—paraphrased from *How to Read a Book* by Mortimer Adler

Fifth Tree

Imagery: The Big Picture from the Small Image

There are some children who love reading and easily comprehend text and all its subtleties.

There are some children who read but struggle to comprehend.

Some who read and comprehend, but don't care about text.

And still others who struggle so hard to decode text that they have no energy left for comprehension.

While each child deserves an individualized approach, there are some overarching principles that apply to all learners.

Here are two universal teaching ideals:

★ Create a means for connecting with text that makes meaning **Visible**.

★ Engage in activities that make comprehension of text **Enjoyable**.

Most of the trees we've climbed thus far have followed this basic tenet: **Visible and Enjoyable**.

Writers make their writing more Visible and Enjoyable by using a familiar word or phrase to symbolize an entire idea. Creating an idea connection can lead to any number of more complex, related associations, helping the reader to comprehend at a deeper level.

For instance, imagine an overscheduled parent saying, "We live in the car." The word *live* is associated with many activities. The statement probably does not mean the family actually *lives* in a car and is homeless (although it can). If the statement is made by a friend who has a home, you know the word *live* is a way of expressing a complex idea by relating it to a familiar concept. By comparing car-time to all of living, we understand the message: *Far too much of my day is spent in the car.* From this the listener can infer the next association: *We are overscheduled.*

This association between a known concept and a particular experience expands our understanding. The deeper connection enlarges the idea and links our thinking to other more Visible themes.

We are going to explore how writers use symbolism to give the reader deeper insight, making their writing Visible and Enjoyable. This insight and imagery makes writing more colorful, so we will use color to illustrate our next lesson.

First let's look at a metaphor about language, to help make our understanding both Visible and Enjoyable. I asked Tracy to paint me a **Language Tree** as a visual metaphor for all that our brains manage both above and below the surface of text.

For my illustration, language is linked with a tree because this familiar image leads to more known associations: roots, soil, trunk, sap, leaves, canopy, etc. So let's explore this metaphor of the Language Tree.

In my Language Tree, the trunk of the tree represents our basic language system, broken into four parts: speaking, listening, reading, and writing. Although language is one living system, it is like a multi-trunked tree—separate yet still a part of the whole. Virginia Berninger breaks our language system into the following components:

- Language by Mouth (speaking)
- Language by Ear (listening)
- Language by Eye (reading)
- Language by Hand (writing)

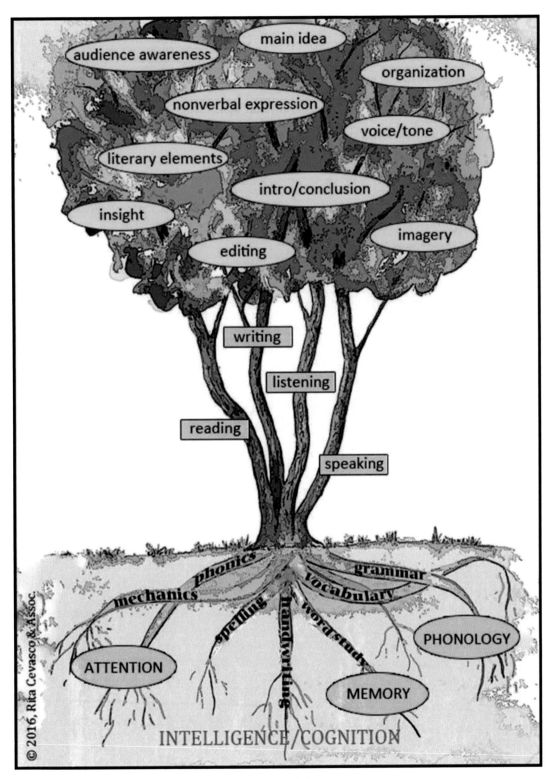

Language Tree.

The canopy of the tree is where deep meaning and comprehension reside. Writers use many techniques to convey their ideas to their readers in an effort to make important themes both Visible and Enjoyable. One of these techniques is imagery, which includes figurative language, sensory connection, and symbolism.

In my Language Tree metaphor, the canopy outlines some aspects referred to as literary elements and rhetorical devices. This is where the color of the tree reveals itself, alive and creative. Deep reading unveils these nuances within a story.

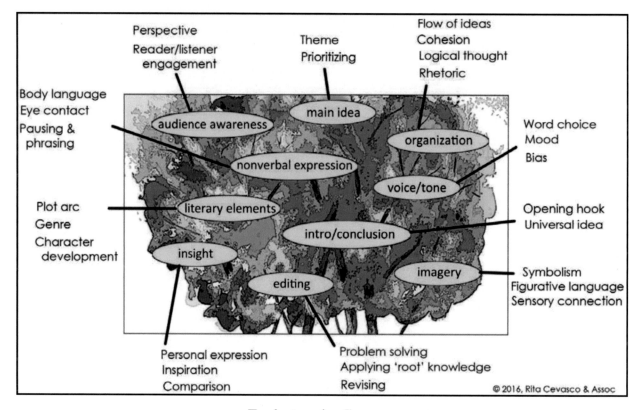

Exploring the Canopy.

We are going to explore the canopy of language in our passage to make one aspect of imagery Visible and Enjoyable: symbolism. We will do this using an activity we call **Colors of the Canopy.**

Celebrating Life's Colors

Writers use symbolic language and imagery to help readers connect. Noticing colorful imagery within stories gives us greater appreciation for the writer. Writers prompt our associations to help us link the story to our own lives.

Let's begin our exploration of the Colors of the Canopy in another passage from *The Invention of Wings* by Sue Monk Kidd.

In the following passage, Sarah has walked into her room to discover Hetty (or Handful) taking a bath in her tub.

Sarah is shocked and angry, yet simultaneously worried that her mother will discover this violation and brutally punish Hetty. While Sarah intellectually encourages defiance of all slave practices, she is afraid to push too far outside of the norms to fight for her ideals. Hetty, by contrast, is growing increasingly angry and bold—ready to fight for herself.

The Invention of Wings by Sue Monk Kidd

Character: Sarah, in conversation with Hetty

She said, "You want me to empty the water out now or wait?"

"Let's do it now. We can't have Mother wander in and find it."

With effort, I helped her roll the sloshing tub through the jib door onto the piazza, close to the rail, hoping the family was inside now and wouldn't hear the gush of water. Handful yanked open the vent and it spilled in a long, silver beak over the side. I seemed to taste it in my mouth, the tang of minerals.

"I know you're angry, Sarah, but I didn't see any harm with me being in the tub, same as you."

Not *Miss* Sarah, but Sarah. I would never again hear her put Miss before my name.

She had the look of someone who'd declared herself, and seeing it, my indignation collapsed and her mutinous bath turned into something else entirely. She'd immersed herself in forbidden privileges, yes, but mostly in the belief she was worthy of those privileges.

Let's begin our **Colors of the Canopy** activity.

Fill in each section of the canopy using the following guideline for interpreting the passage; write your answers in the numbered areas of the tree's canopy. Notice that you are only writing your ideas in **Bits and Pieces,** so that you do not have to feel intimidated. Find words that speak to you, provoking images **In My Head.** Use the directions below.

How to Teach This Lesson to your Children:

Using the passage provided and the Colors of the Canopy sheet, answer these questions on the corresponding numbered lines:

1. *Find and copy a metaphor or simile.*

2. *Explain how the metaphor or simile enhances the story's plot, the character, or the setting.*

3. *Find three words or phrases that evoke a sensory response, of either seeing, hearing, touching, smelling, or tasting.*

4. *Describe your response to this passage.*

5. *Make a prediction about what will happen next in the story.*

6. *Copy your favorite sentence or phrase in the passage.*

Exploring text with simple guided questions helps to make ideas more **Visible and Enjoyable** to the reader. You can introduce the **Colors of the Canopy** exercise to your children using the activity pages and passages in Appendix A and B.

Connecting Language to Language Arts ✺ Narrowing the Focus

Guided questions can help us narrow our focus on key aspects of text—in this case, symbolism. A narrow focus actually helps us to converge on an idea, going deeper into meaning. This is in direct contrast to brainstorming, which encourages us to diverge by spreading out our thoughts—thinking broadly, but not deeply.

Dissecting text in Intentional Copywork separates it into defined parts, helping children discover key literary devices. Because symbolism is quite common in fiction, a deep comprehension thinker learns to watch for symbolic language, making note of its related ideas.

In this exercise, we practice many skills needed in future writing tasks: finding meaningful quotes and noting our responses In My Head.

—Rita

"Not just to passively read, but to fully enter a text... to mingle with an author."

—Sam Anderson

Colors of the Canopy

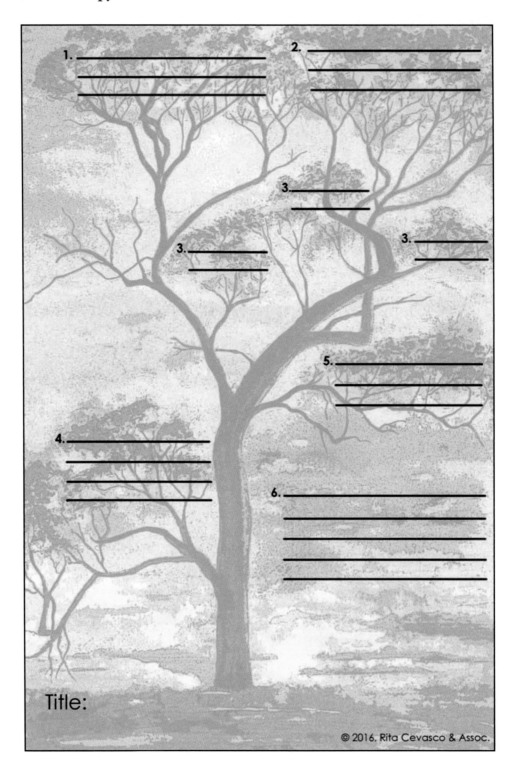

1. _____
_____
_____

2. _____
_____
_____

3. _____
_____

3. _____
_____

3. _____
_____

5. _____
_____
_____

4. _____
_____
_____
_____

6. _____
_____
_____
_____
_____

Title:

Here are two student samples from the poem *Circles* by Myra Cohn Livingston.

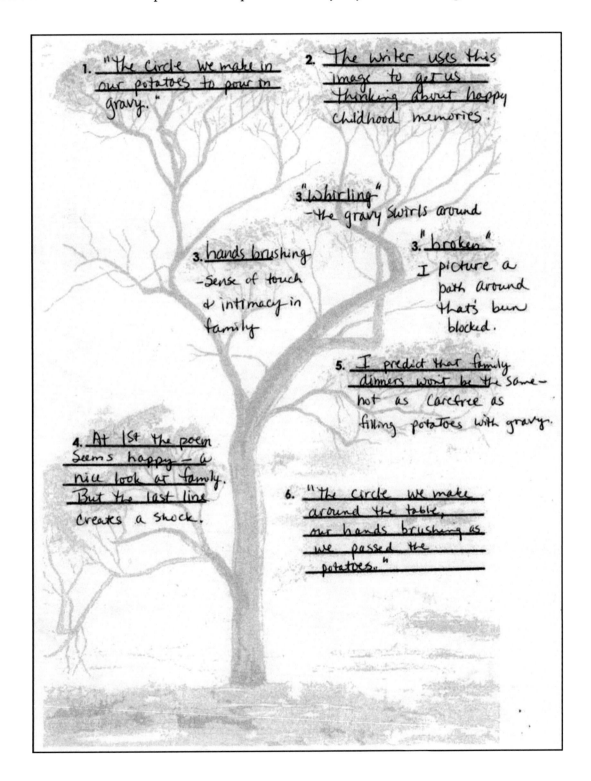

1. "The circle we make in our potatoes to pour in gravy."

2. The writer uses this image to get us thinking about happy childhood memories.

3. "whirling"
   —the gravy swirls around

3. "broken"
   I picture a path around that's been blocked.

3. hands brushing
   —Sense of touch & intimacy in family

5. I predict that family dinners won't be the same— not as carefree as filling potatoes with gravy.

4. At 1st the poem seems happy — a nice look at family. But the last line creates a shock.

6. "the circle we make around the table, our hands brushing as we passed the potatoes."

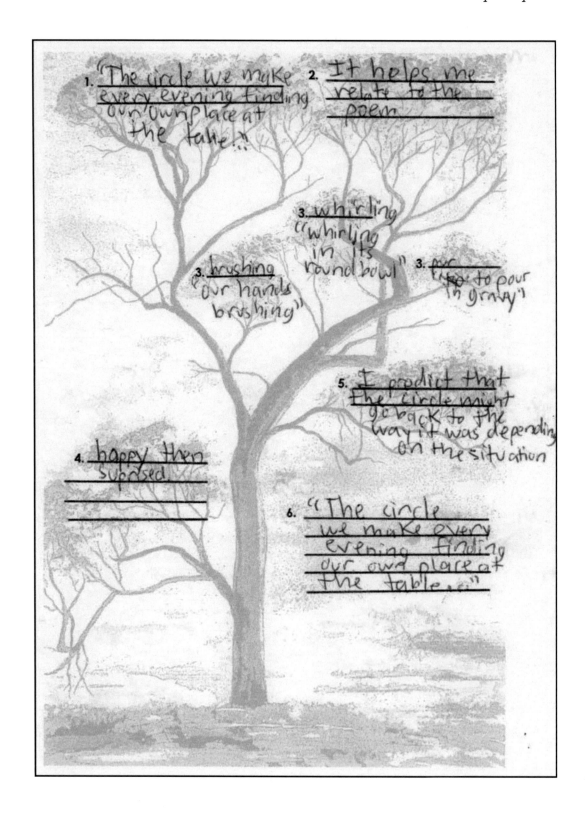

1. "The circle we make every evening finding our own place at the table."

2. It helps me relate to the poem

3. whirling "whirling in its round bowl"

3. brushing "our hands brushing"

3. our "____ to pour in gravy"

5. I predict that the circle might go back to the way it was depending on the situation

4. happy then suprised

6. "The circle we make every evening finding our own place at the table."

Connecting Language to Language Arts ✦ Visible and Enjoyable

I like to compare reading and writing with dancing. I am not good at motor planning, so I need explicit dance instruction that shows each step slowly—practiced over and over—and still more practice putting steps together. But a natural dancer, with naturally strong coordination and motor planning skills, learns basic steps easily without explicit training, then consolidates those steps into a fluent routine. The strong dancer who easily masters a repertoire is free to improvise. Improvisation brings forth innovative ideas that inspire us all.

My students who struggle the most teach me how to teach. The struggling student does not have the skills needed to gain automaticity in some or all reading and writing skills: decoding, spelling, handwriting, writing conventions, written expression and reading comprehension. So I must learn the best ways to teach each student. We must practice the steps as well as the entire dance routine.

Students who struggle remind me that my teaching needs to be both **Visible and Enjoyable**:

Visible because children who struggle in any given area will not easily make connections to text and writing. They struggle to gain automaticity, so they must learn each step explicitly. Each Visible skill needs to be practiced repeatedly, both in isolation and in connection with other related skills. Repeated skill practice is by nature a dull affair, yet for many children, it cannot be avoided.

Enjoyable because struggling learners spend entire school days engaging in tasks that are difficult and frustrating. They struggle with cognitive fatigue and feelings of shame or embarrassment. Sometimes anger and resentment result. The more we can make skill practice Enjoyable, the easier it is on everyone. As in my dance metaphor, music that I enjoy inspires me to overcome my awkwardness in dancing. If I don't like the music, I tend to sit on the sideline and watch. Or I find something else to do.

(continued)

Connecting Language to Language Arts ✹ Visible and Enjoyable

(continued)

More than anything, learning that is Enjoyable supports the parent-child bond—a bond often challenged when reading and writing difficulties define the day.

Children with stronger reading and writing skills also benefit from teaching that is Visible and Enjoyable. They naturally create reading and writing games because their skills help them to explore with joy. They improvise and then innovate, much like a dancer. Their innovative ideas can be borrowed and modified, to the benefit of all. We want to use creative ideas to encourage our children's sense of fun. Then we can sit back and enjoy the language-rich play they create.

—Rita

"Just because you've seen something doesn't mean you'll stop looking. There's always something you didn't see before."

—from *Time Cat* by Lloyd Alexander

Sixth Tree

A Feeling of Place

When I look at this painting by Tracy, I feel drawn in. I have never been to this place, yet I have been to similar places. However, my response is not about the beach or ocean. This painting evokes memories in me of this *type* of place—in other words, I experience a **Feeling of Place**.

I see this painting, and I am reminded of vacation. Not my fit-in-every-site-while-traveling-around-major-cities vacations, but my perfect-balance-of-discovery-and-peaceful-relaxation vacations. I have been here, in this Feeling of Place, even though I have not been there, the actual location of the painting.

Readers must sense the Feeling of Place in a story in order to dive deeply into meaning. We readers may never have been in the exact story's location, or even the story's time period, yet we know or can imagine a similar place in our minds. More importantly, because we live in the world of humankind, we know the story's place in our hearts as well.

We are going to write in Bits and Pieces about place in the novel, *The Invention of Wings*. The best way to write in Bits and Pieces is to do a series of short freewrites. Freewriting allows us to let our thoughts flow, giving us permission to write. This is private writing. We put our pens to paper and just write thoughts. We can start and end in the middle of our thinking. We are free from spelling or grammar concerns or any obligation to be precise. Freewriting engages us in writing that is free of any concerns beyond that which is In My Head. It is a means of capturing thoughts, but also of elaborating thoughts, or even clarifying thoughts. Sometimes, freewriting leads to the discovery of thoughts.

Just as Tracy knows the subject and mood she intends to paint, as in the beach painting opposite, she may still uncover an unexpected Feeling of Place in the finished piece. Likewise, when we freewrite, we know the subject we intend to write about, but we reveal new perspectives In My Head as we write.

This freewriting exercise involves short three-minute segments of writing that help us look from different angles at a single topic. In this way, we are able to both elaborate and dig deeper. Remember, the ability to dig deeper is needed to elaborate—we need to converge on an idea in order to explore its complexities.

We are going to explore the setting of *The Invention of Wings* because it serves as a microcosm of the whole world of humankind. In this book, because the story is historical fiction, we know the setting represents a particular time and place in history: America in the 1800s before the Civil War, when slavery was legal in the South. Each short freewrite will help us explore what a single setting in the story represents about the time period, as well as all of humankind, especially today.

We will set a timer and write for three minutes on each prompt, keeping pen or pencil moving, even if we are unsure what to write. For example, I can write, "I am not sure if this means…"

Whatever is In My Head will be written in the freewrite. After completing each freewrite, we read it aloud and listen to our own words. We can add any additional thoughts at this point. Then move to the next prompt, set the timer for another three minutes, write, and read aloud again.

Writing in three-minute segments is most helpful when we read our writing with another person engaged in the same task. When we share our writing by reading aloud, we mimic turn-taking in conversation. In conversation what another person says influences our next thought. When I write three-minute freewrites with students, we take turns reading to each other, commenting on our thoughts and Bits and Pieces of writing. Then we continue writing, stopping and discussing after each bit of writing. Taking turns helps us explore a topic in a way similar to conversation. By reading aloud, Bits and Pieces of writing lead us deeper into meaning.

Before we begin, here is a sample of my writing with a student. I am careful not to overwhelm children with my adult-level ideas, so I keep my ideas simple and my writing evenly-paced with their speed and comprehension level. **Shared Writing** helps learners connect more fully with the broader themes in a story.

A story's setting inspires conversation about our larger world. Writing with a Feeling of Place focuses on setting to make connections with greater, universal ideas.

Laurie's Journal

With Nemo and Sigourney I have commonly used setting immersion to great benefit. For example, so much classic literature involves horses and sailing that I signed them up for lessons in these areas due to the foreignness of the vocabulary. In Black Beauty, *what is a martingale? What does it feel like to tack into the wind or to sail alone? I generally try to take a story and attend to the setting in some way. I love the idea of investigating why authors choose the settings they do.*

The following is a writing sample of Shared Writing about the humorous children's picture book, *Cinder Edna* by Ellen Jackson. Together, a 13-year-old student and I discussed Edna's world.

From Edna's world, we each wrote for three minutes on how the story reminds us of the whole world of people. For many children, this concept is a challenge. By engaging in Shared Writing —sharing our freewrites and reading them aloud to each other—this student was able to connect to broader, common themes about human nature.

Once the connection to the whole world was made, via our Shared Writing, with my writing influencing her ideas and her writing influencing mine, this young student was able to grasp a universal view. Once she had a universal view of how the story relates to humankind, she was able to write on a more personal level. Her personal connection helped her gain insight.

2

Rita's Journal–Like the Whole World

In America, there are those who are wealthy—they can choose to be frivolous or learn to be productive people. They don't have to work. The Cinders represent the people who have to work. They can choose to feel resentful, living life always wanting more, like Cinderella. Or, they can be productive and content like CinderEdna, knowing that people, not money, will make them happy.

1

Journaling Together–Edna's World

A small village in a kingdom. There are peasants who work, and there is a castle with two princes. Everyone wears modern clothes.

3

Student Journal–Like My World

Cinder Edna is the most like me. She is always working cheerfully. Although I wouldn't say I work cheerfully all the time. She also saves up for what she wants. That is also the same thing that I have to do . . . Edna never complained about having to take the bus, but we sometimes do.

Let's explore our Feeling of Place from *The Invention of Wings*. Because this activity works best when we take turns in writing, we are going to do this together. In order to create a Shared Writing experience, I will share my writing with you. We will begin with one of the book's settings—the house in Charleston.

Wonderful literature inspires me to carry a story around In My Head, even without realizing it. Then, when I am in a location, I have that sense—a Feeling of Place—that resonates with a story I've read. This happened to me with *The Invention of Wings*. I was in Charleston, South Carolina in 2015, and visited some of the mansions there. I immediately began to imagine Sarah's home (which was also Hetty's prison). Because I read the book, I was more interested in my surroundings, so I have pictures to share now.

Here is a typical home of a wealthy land and slave owner who lived in the early 1800s across the street from the ocean. Notice the verandas. Long porches helped to cool the house and welcomed the ocean breezes.

I found a walled yard, similar to the "whole map of the world" that kept Hetty enclosed.

This barn also had slave quarters above the animals. Unlike Hetty's room, these at least have windows.

From the photos, we can jot down some ideas about the house in Charleston:

Charleston House

Sarah's house is large and imposing. It has the best of everything for her day. She has many porches on all levels of the house. There is a large walled yard that holds the kitchen rooms and the stables. Slaves live above these outbuildings. The kitchen is hot and the stable smells of manure.

You can try this for yourself—jot a few ideas about the Charleston House setting using the circles here or provided in Appendix A.

Charleston House

Now you will write for three minutes on how the Charleston house is a microcosm of the whole world—in this case, America before the Civil War. Remember the writer uses setting as a platform for developing character, creating plot, and exploring themes. Let the setting act as a launching pad for your own thoughts as well. You may find yourself writing about well-known themes of slavery, socio-economic levels, fairness, etc.

Now read both your writing and my sample. Think about how each of us expressed our understanding of the larger world, and therefore, the overarching *message* about humankind.

Like the Whole World

Like the Whole World

Sarah lives in a house with comforts that she could not have without a slave. Her bath requires hours of hauling water, her fireplace burns throughout the night, and her chamber pot must be emptied. Without slaves, all of these luxuries would be chores or expenses. Hetty is given a room that represents her sub-human status—a stall in the barn. She is property and must sleep outside Sarah's room on the floor. She is valued for her work. She must meet every whim of her owners. Slaves allowed the rich to avoid work. In America, slaves were exploited to maintain a wealthy lifestyle. People who exploit others do so because they let their own needs rule.

Next you will write for three minutes on how the larger world reminds you of your own world. You may find yourself applying the themes of the book to your own life—drawing similarities or differences.

When you are done, read both freewrites aloud. Hopefully, sharing our freewrites added to your depth of discovery.

Like My World

Like My World

I sit in my own house and observe
my comforts: heating and air conditioning,
electricity, an attached bath with running water,
flush toilets, and two cars in my garage. My refrigerator
and cupboards filled with food—food that may expire
before it's eaten. Bedrooms with beds that are now empty,
waiting for the few times a year my adult children return
home. The human cost for all of this is also in this house, but
hidden from view. I don't have slaves sleeping outside my
bedroom door. Yet there is human suffering attached to
everything. Workers with low wages or long hours, an
environment that suffers from my outlets connected
to multiple electronics, cars that pollute. I could
make changes to my life to alter this, but I
would have to give up my current
comfort level.

Exploring setting may seem like the most tedious of comprehension strategies, yet writers carefully select settings as a springboard for telling stories. Writers know they cannot write about an entire world, so they write about a smaller world to serve as a microcosm of our own lives. Even writers like Tolkien, who create other worlds, understand that they are creating a parallel or extension of the world we inhabit.

The idea of exploring microcosms in young children's literature is nicely explained in the book *Deconstructing Penguins* by Lawrence and Nancy Goldstone. The Goldstones help children discover setting by asking questions. While asking questions is a useful tool, it is important to ask opinion-based questions that have no right answer. However, when we *write* as a means of discovery, we then share our writing as a catalyst for discussion. We invite our children to think of more than one answer. We invite them to become deep thinkers—reflective about human nature and about their own lives.

When we explore a Feeling of Place, we explore thoughts on both the larger world and our own smaller lives.

"Reading is the only true form of time travel..."

—Claire Molitors

Feeling of Place ✸ *Blart—A Little Blob of Art* by Tracy Molitors

The simpler the setting, the better the platform for conveying parallels with the larger world. The reader is free to find connections without interference from unfamiliar elements when setting is reduced to its very essence. For this reason, our children will explore a **Feeling of Place** using a picture book with a simple setting: *Blart—A Little Blob of Art* by Tracy Molitors. Blart lives within Tracy's art journal on his own blank page, so children can make associations freely. When I introduce *Blart*, students of all ages find him Enjoyable.

Blart—A Little Blob of Art reminds me of the theory of *negative space*, a theory Tracy taught my children in art class. Because Blart lives on a blank page, his empty world encourages a more Visible perspective—or insight—into our own.

Connecting Art to Language Arts ✸ Negative Space

As we enjoy and study the art around us, we tend to observe the obvious shapes and figures. We are drawn to the colors and lines that artists seem to create so effortlessly. But what we often miss are the empty spaces—areas where nothing is painted or drawn. This is what artists call the negative space. It might sound boring, but it can be the difference between a good picture and a great one. Negative or empty space can be the thing that causes a line to pop out. It can change the perspective of a piece—making a figure appear larger or smaller, busy or bored, surrounded or lonely.

Look at Blart's story with an eye to the negative space. How does the white page define Blart's world? How does it influence your feelings about Blart as a character? How would your connection to Blart be different without the negative space?

—Tracy

Enjoy *Blart—A Little Blob of Art*, and then begin to freewrite on the microcosm of Blart's world, and what it tells us about the whole world of people, as well as our own lives. Complete your freewrites on the page provided. Consider sharing Blart and this freewriting exercise with your children using the directions and activity pages in Appendix A.

How to Teach This Lesson to your Children:

*Let's explore the **Feeling of Place** in Blart's world from* Blart—A Little Blob of Art. *Jot a few ideas about the setting of the story:*

Blart's World

When we share writing, we inspire each other to deeper and deeper insights. Here are some ideas my students wrote in the Blart exercise:

Blart's World

Blart's world is a drawing in a book. It is page to page.

Blart's World

It is a sketch pad

It has 5 characters

It is mostly blank pages

Now let's compare Blart's World to the Whole World of People. Think of some things about Blart that remind you of your city, your country, or your planet.

Like the Whole World

Like the Whole World

Blart wants a friend. However, when he accidently makes baby-blarts of art, he runs away. Is it because he's scared or because he's too timid to approach or confront the baby-blarts? It is probably both. Blart is similar to the way people try to obtain friends.

Like the Whole World

Blart runs away because he's scared… Blart comes back to save the little ones. The little ones follow because they most likely look up to him… Some people help each other. Once they help each other, they get along.

Compare Blart's World to your world. Think of some things about Blart that remind you of your family, friends, school, or neighborhood.

Like My World

Like My World

This is like when I went to Guatemala. I went somewhere new, and then I met new people and I played with the little ones. Then they started to like me. At first I was shy… then we played soccer together and things got less strange after a while.

Like My World

Like Blart, there are two different ways I treat people when I meet them. One way, I'm hostile, and the other mode of greeting is friendly and nice… These two different ways of meeting people are normally how I treat them when I first meet them.

Like My World

Blart is like myself because I'm not big on new people and things, but if I can help I will, like when I met Elise. I didn't know what to talk about at first, but then after a while, we became good friends.

Exploring a Feeling of Place

We have a natural desire to connect with other times and places. Our children create play spaces of imaginative little worlds—sometimes mimicking the real, such as playing house, pretending to camp, or playing spy. Children also create new worlds in their play, such as fairy lands, monster dens, superhero worlds, and magical hideaways.

Taking time to explore the microcosms of stories enriches our imagination, and therefore, our deep understanding of text. Using online images is another way to help us map out a story's progression, allowing us to imagine what we cannot visit.

For example, seeing the various houses in movie versions of Jane Austen's book, *Pride and Prejudice*, helps the reader to better understand the theme that women of the day were essentially trying to find a house to shelter them, and the only way to secure this goal was through marriage. The various houses and their reflective social strata helped to drive home the plight of Elizabeth and her sisters: if they didn't find a husband with a house, even an unwelcoming mansion filled with distasteful people, they would be homeless.

Rita's daughter Emma reads
***Sacagawea* and visits
Ft. Clatsop, Oregon.**

As parents we help our children link the microcosms from story to their play. As we discuss story settings in relation to their toys, dress-up clothes, art and props, we heighten the connection between story setting and their own world. We show them the power of setting in their own verbal play and writing.

Wonderful literature inspires children to create their own worlds in original stories. When Nemo and Sigourney became enamored of the book *Redwall*, they created their own animal worlds. They began to see setting as the launching pad for their ideas. By focusing on a story's setting, our exploration of the Feeling of Place becomes a launching pad for our own.

a snail peacefully slides across the forest floor, when a leaf moves and pushes a haselnut out of the way. suddenly······

Nemo's characters in their habitat.

Seventh Tree

Laying a Path: Deeper Meaning and Richer Comprehension

We began this book by **Laying a Path** to help our children deepen their comprehension while engaging in writing, because reading and writing are interconnected skills that are best learned together. Each aspect of language—by mouth, ear, eye, or hand—is a tangle of entwined abilities that grow together. Strengthening one strengthens all. Everything we learn and teach is best explored through discussion, reading, and writing.

When we engage our children in rich discussion of ideas, we strengthen their speaking and listening skills, helping them to consider new ideas and formulate their own. Our language system taps into thinking—thinking that is broadened in response to and in the midst of verbal expression.

Like discussion, reading is another means of expanding our thinking. Reading exposes us to the rich ideas of others. Reading builds new concepts, as well, as we take in new information and respond with our own ideas. Furthermore, writing is an integral part of reading. The more we write, the more we learn about reading, and the more we learn about our own thinking.

Laurie's Journal

The choice of beautiful literature is key. It is passive elevation that inspires us to savor and deepen comprehension—the whole, this-is-why-we-do-it piece—because it IS beautiful and life-enhancing. Sometimes we need to remember something as obvious as why-we-do-it.

All four trunks of the language tree (listening, speaking, reading, and writing) give life to the entire system—as one trunk grows, the whole tree grows.

Connecting Language to Language Arts ✷ Language Needs Time

Language is understood and expressed in all four modalities, by Mouth, by Ear, by Eye, and by Hand, with each mode interconnected, yet thriving on its own. As parents, we understand that our children's speaking began after their listening, but also that our children's speaking enhanced their listening. We know that speaking lags behind listening in early development, but not by much. By three months of age our babies cooed. Their cooing led to babbling, and their babbling led to words, all in about a year's time. Our babies played with sounds and words, and through all their verbal play, their listening skills improved as well. The connections between speaking and listening are constantly growing in our children, and in ourselves, throughout our lifetimes.

In the same way, reading and writing are interconnected and need time to grow. We don't wait on reading before beginning writing. Nor do we expect writing to emerge fully developed, no more than we expect full sentences to emerge from our babies.

—Rita

Intentional Copywork, in which we read, discuss, write, discuss, and read the text again, strengthens learning for each literary passage that our children study. As they dig deeply into one piece of text, a Tree, children gain understanding and learn skills that help them to master language in all its forms, the Forest.

We have walked together on this path of exploring and expressing our responses to text, experiencing the important links between listening, speaking, reading, and writing for ourselves. We have helped our children interact with passages and simple stories along the way. We have heightened our children's awareness of which aspects of a passage are worthy of notice, helping them to engage in thinking, not just about the story, but the larger world.

Now, we are going to ask our children to write in direct response to reading, engaging in the **On the Page/In My Head** exercise that you practiced at the beginning of this book. By now, our children will be aware of what we mean by In My Head thinking. They are beginning to understand that a reader reacts and interacts with text. They have a heightened awareness of the role imagery plays in helping them to associate ideas—what is On the Page joining with what they know of life.

Some parents find selecting a passage to be a challenge. Ideas about selecting a passage can be found in the box Connecting Language to Language Arts: Selecting a Passage. You have many options from which to choose:

✸ In Appendix B you will find multiple passages for this exercise. You may have used these passages before, but no matter—reusing a passage enhances a child's ability to do this task.

✸ Choose a passage that best fits your child's reading and interest level. For this exercise do not worry if the passage is unfamiliar. Unfamiliarity has its advantages as well. When children read an unknown passage, they may be more sensitive to the text. They pay closer attention to what is On the Page, in order to understand how to interpret with In My Head thoughts.

✸ As another option, select a passage from a book your child is currently reading. When children are fully engaged in a story, this is also advantageous. Children broaden their In My Head thinking to include the whole scope of the story, embellishing On the Page details.

Be aware that having prior knowledge of the story has one set of advantages and having no prior knowledge has another set of advantages, so you may want to spend a few weeks on this activity, trying both types of passage selections. Hopefully you will use this exercise at least once a month in your language arts program, using passages from literature your children are reading.

You can find the **On the Page/In My Head** directions and journal pages in Appendix A. Children can write in their own writing journals as well. Student samples of this activity can be found in Appendix C.

Connecting Language to Language Arts ✸ Selecting a Passage

Picking a passage can feel daunting, but a few simple guidelines can help. Select a passage that includes one of the following elements:

Introduction—an opening hook or description of setting or character from the first few chapters of the book

Conflict—a representation of the main conflict within the story

Point of View—a demonstration of the narrative style

Symbolism or Imagery—similes, metaphors, personification, or other language that stimulates the imagination

Theme—a representation of the theme or common motifs in the story

Dialogue—a demonstration of character traits and the conventions of dialogue punctuation

Climax—an important turning point in the story

Resolution—a final paragraph or a passage that shows character development

Interest—stylistic forms in the story including poetry, humor, foreshadowing, or tone, etc.

—*Rita*

Important Modifications to Remember:

- ✦ Spread this activity over a few days for children who are overwhelmed by the act of writing.

- ✦ Share the writing with your children, just as I did with Nemo. Take turns with your struggling writer, helping them by writing either a portion of the passage On the Page or a portion of their In My Head thoughts.

- ✦ Ensure that your child works only to a level of success, not frustration—always. Use your best judgment for each child, and don't be afraid to modify the lesson by reducing the length of the passage or by choosing an easier passage than the current grade level.

- ✦ Remember, the best Intentional Copywork practice uses literature children can read accurately and independently.

Connecting Language and Art to Language Arts ✳
Annotation and Marginalia

To encourage children to interact with text, educators use a method known as *annotation*. Annotating text involves marking up passages to draw attention to key details, important facts, main ideas, and reader responses. The word *annotating* means to add notes to the text. I like to call it **Reading with a Pencil**. Reading with a Pencil is the act of writing In My Head thoughts in the margins. [See Appendix C for a student sample.] George Steiner once defined an intellectual as, "quite simply, a human being who has a pencil in his or her hand when reading a book."

When children engage in In My Head practice, annotating becomes easier. Once they internalize In My Head thinking, they can begin to write in the margins of their books. Writing in books is a good thing. Just make sure to write lightly and use a good eraser for library books!

Reading with a Pencil is a form of the **In My Head/On the Page** activity that we did with *This Is Not My Hat*. In Reading with a Pencil, we annotate in the margins instead of on Post-it Notes.

Marginalia, or notes written, scribbled, or drawn in the margins of a book or document, have been around for as long as books. Many people collect marginalia for their beauty or interest, sometimes paying thousands of dollars to read the thoughts of famous people who have written in books authored by others.

 In medieval times marginalia were often pictorial. Bibles were filled with small pictures in the margins illustrating various aspects of the text. Marginalia served both to explain the text and to decorate the book. So doodling in the margins is a time-honored tradition!

The ancient form of marginalia acts as an **In My Head/On the Page** exercise, encouraging readers to react with words or pictures, use Bits and Pieces of writing, and therefore:

✳   evaluate and interpret text more closely,

✳   converse with the text, and

✳   remember what a writer says.

—Rita and Tracy

Language Arts: A Week of Intentional Copywork

All the activities in this book are developed for the practice of Intentional Copywork (see page 13). Here are key lessons we learned on our journey together, exploring **Deep Meaning and Comprehension** within the **Forest** of reading and writing.

As we walk this tree-lined trail with our children, we are **Laying a Path** for learning by working to their level of success. Our backpacks are laden with new tools for discovery and adventure.

- ✶ **Bits and Pieces** of writing are worthy activities to grow writers.

- ✶ **Visible and Enjoyable** exercises encourage all of us to engage more deeply with text.

- ✶ **On the Page/In My Head** supports reflective thoughts, close reading, and comprehension.

- ✶ **In My Head/On the Page** is an **Enjoyable** form of **Reading with a Pencil** for annotation and marginalia.

- ✶ **On the Floor/On the Stage** play, **Drawing Is Seeing** cartooning, and **Phrase Trees** give children time to engage with stories and the means to connect stories with their world.

- ✶ **A Feeling of Place** is a focused writing activity encouraging children to connect stories to broader themes.

Children who engage with text think on a level that builds analytical skills over time. Strong readers have this in common: they connect intimately with writing as they interact with text.

Typical **Intentional Copywork** includes four separate passage selections from the same story over the course of a month. When we take one book a month and dig deeply into the text, using these practices, we are studying a **Tree** to learn the **Forest** of written works within our world, and hopefully, within ourselves.

We want to spend an entire week on a passage, growing intimate with both its meaning and the writer's voice. We want to use all our language skills—spoken conversation, listening, reading, and writing—as vehicles for understanding and sharing the words of others. Intimacy with text promotes a culture of appreciation that may ignite into a passion.

Investigating meaning, conversing with text, and connecting the writer's words to our own lives strengthens our higher-level thinking skills: observation, understanding, abstraction, analysis, and symbolic representation. But it also increases our emotional response: how we react and interact with word choice, quotations, characters, plot twists, etc. When we dig deeply into text, we dig deeply into ourselves as well.

So what does a week of **Intentional Copywork** look like?

In the preface I introduced the teaching model: *I do it (parent). We do it (parent and child). You do it (child).* However, in **Intentional Copywork** with struggling readers and writers, the teaching model may follow this pattern: *I do it. We do it. We do it. We do it . . . You do it.* A week of **Intentional Copywork** begins with deep meaning and comprehension, including the activities within this book.

Each month, over the course of your school year, these activities can be used with copywork passages. We recommend using **On the Page/In My Head** at least once a month and the other activities in between. Different passages resonate with different exercises, so you can pick and choose for the best fit.

Suggested Weekly Plan

Monday	**Deep meaning and comprehension**
I do it	Select a passage (or select with your child) to use throughout the week.
We do it	Read passage together and discuss it within the context of the book. Focus on meaning, discussing big ideas from the canopy.
	Engage in one of the activities from the book: **On the Page/In My Head, In My Head/On the Page, Cartooning Characters, Phrase Trees, Colors of the Canopy,** or **Feeling of Place.**
You do it	Engage in **Bits and Pieces** of writing to connect with and analyze the text.
	Take time for **On the Floor/On the Stage** activities throughout the week.
Tuesday	**Phonics, spelling, word study, and vocabulary**
I do it	Select words from the same passage and create a phonics, spelling, and vocabulary lesson.
We do it	Use *Trees in the Forest* future editions for activities or incorporate your own phonics, spelling, and vocabulary programs.
You do it	Engage in **Bits and Pieces** of writing to practice target words and phrases from the text.
Wednesday	**Grammar, punctuation, and handwriting**
I do it	Look at the text and create a grammar and punctuation lesson. Use *Trees in the Forest* future editions for activities or incorporate your own grammar program.
We do it	Read the week's passage together, emphasizing the grammar lesson. Notice and discuss punctuation.
You do it	Engage in **Bits and Pieces** of writing to practice grammatically complex sentences using good handwriting.

Thursday	**Intentional Copywork and Intentional Editing**
I do it	Once again, review and practice phonics, spelling, and punctuation.
You do it	Copy the passage using best handwriting.
We do it	Edit together and correct errors.
Friday	**Dictation and Intentional Editing**
We do it	Review based on copywork errors.
	Dictate passage while your child writes.
	Edit together.
You do it	Share **On the Floor/On the Stage** activities with your family.

Intentional Copywork is *intentional* for both you and your child.

The intentional parent

- attends to the child's reading and writing level,
- selects a passage from a current piece of literature,
- creates mini-lessons based on literary content, and
- focuses on child-centered skill training.

The intentional child

- notices the text and its relationship to self,
- practices **In My Head** thinking for deep comprehension,
- engages in skill-based lessons related to literature,
- connects with text through **Visible and Enjoyable** activities, and
- consolidates skills in writing.

Intentional Language Arts

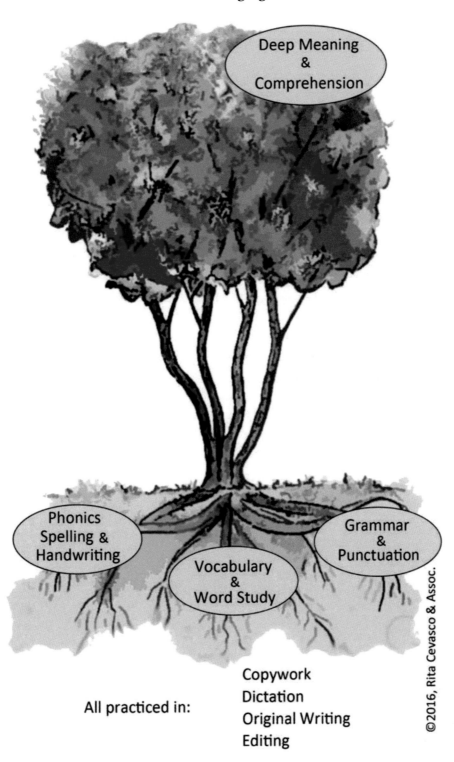

Deep Meaning & Comprehension

Phonics Spelling & Handwriting

Vocabulary & Word Study

Grammar & Punctuation

All practiced in:

Copywork
Dictation
Original Writing
Editing

©2016, Rita Cevasco & Assoc.

We have been on a long journey together, examining Trees to help us understand this vast Forest we call literature. We have climbed up into the canopy to comprehend deep meaning within text and to enter into the writer's world. We have engaged in Bits and Pieces of writing to help us become writers ourselves.

We have enjoyed passages, engaging with meaning in text to prepare for weekly Intentional Copywork with our children. We have learned to use activities, such as On the Page/In My Head or Phrase Trees, to augment copywork once or twice a month. We use the ideas in this book again and again to study Trees.

We would like our language arts to spill over into our children's creative play, so that some books will stimulate a multitude of adventures. More than anything, we want to inspire a lifelong love of literature.

As we climb each Tree, we encourage those around us to keep lists of all the books explored, identifying individual and family favorites. We celebrate much-loved stories.

There are many other aspects of *studying a Tree to learn the Forest*, but we have begun this journey by examining the essence of *why* we read and *why* we write: to engage in meaningful conversation through text.

So, let's keep climbing Trees…

APPENDIX A

On the Page/In my Head Instructions

Here are instructions to reference when doing this exercise in the future:

Everyone has different experiences with the exercise **On the Page/ In My Head**. *You may think of relating with text as a habit you take for granted, or you may discover that this is a new skill to master.*

As you do your copywork, you are going to separate your writing into two columns. On the left side, you will first copy the passage—the words on the page, verbatim. We call this side **On the Page**, *and it is typical copywork.*

Once you have completed a section of the copywork on the left side, stopping at a natural break in the passage, you will then proceed to the right side of the paper. In this column, you will write the messages and clues the writer is conveying to you. You will interpret the meaning of this portion of the passage, as well as your own thoughts, reactions, and feelings. We call this **In My Head** *because you are revealing your side of an intimate conversation between you and the writer.*

Continue copying the passage **On the Page,** *one portion at a time. At the end of each section, stop and capture your thoughts* **In My Head** *on the right side.*

Remember: because you are interpreting meaning—what we call inferencing—as well as your thoughts and feelings, there is no exact answer. While it is possible to misinterpret a message, everyone's thoughts and feelings are valid, no matter how they differ.

APPENDIX A

On The Page/ In My Head— Important Modifications to Consider:

★ Spread this activity over a few days for children who are overwhelmed by the act of writing.

★ Share the writing with your children. Take turns with your struggling writer, helping them by writing either a portion of the passage or a portion of their thoughts.

★ Ensure that your child works only to a level of success, not frustration—always. Use your best judgment for each child, and don't be afraid to modify the lesson by reducing the length of the passage or by choosing a passage appropriate to your child's reading level.

★ Remember, the best **Intentional Copywork** practice uses literature children can accurately read independently, so choose a passage from one of their books.

APPENDIX A

On the Page/In my Head Journal Page

On The Page   In My Head

APPENDIX A

Influential Books Journal Page

Influential Books in my Life	How These Books Influenced Me

APPENDIX A

A Feeling of Place Shared Writing Instructions

Here are directions to reference when doing this exercise with your children:

When we talk in conversation, we pick a topic, taking turns talking and listening to each other. Let's write just like we talk, taking turns reading and listening to each other's ideas. We are going to have a writing conversation!

Let's do 3 short freewrites, taking turns each time, just like when we talk.

Freewrite One: *Let's explore our story's world. We will each write for 3 minutes about the setting. We are writing inside circles because the setting represents this story's whole world. Let's set the timer and write.*

Thanks for writing for 3 minutes! Who wants to read their writing first? After the first reader, each listener will make one positive comment on one or more of the ideas presented. Let's continue sharing until we each have a chance to read our writing aloud. By sharing writing, we inspire each other.

Freewrite Two: *Now let's write for another 3 minutes. In this circle we will each compare our story's world to the Whole World of People. Think of some things about our story that remind you of your city, country, or planet. Set the timer again.*

Thanks for writing for 3 more minutes! Who wants to read first this time? Each listener will again make one positive comment on the ideas presented. Let's notice how each of us expresses our ideas about the world and how our story inspires our understanding of human nature.

Freewrite Three: *Now that we have explored our story's message about people, let's write for a final 3 minutes, this time comparing our story's world to our personal world. Think of things that remind you of family, friends, school, or neighborhood. What does the book's message show us about our lives? Set the timer again.*

Thanks for writing one last time! Now let's read to each other a final time, sharing our thoughts and making positive comments. It is nice to appreciate each other's insights and hear what others think about our own writing.

APPENDIX A

A Feeling of Place—Like the Story's World

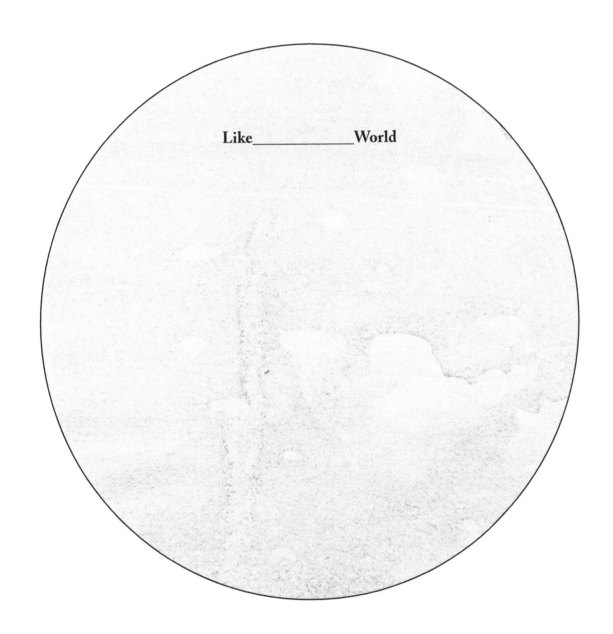

Like_____World

APPENDIX A

A Feeling of Place—Like the Whole World

APPENDIX A

A Feeling of Place—Like My World

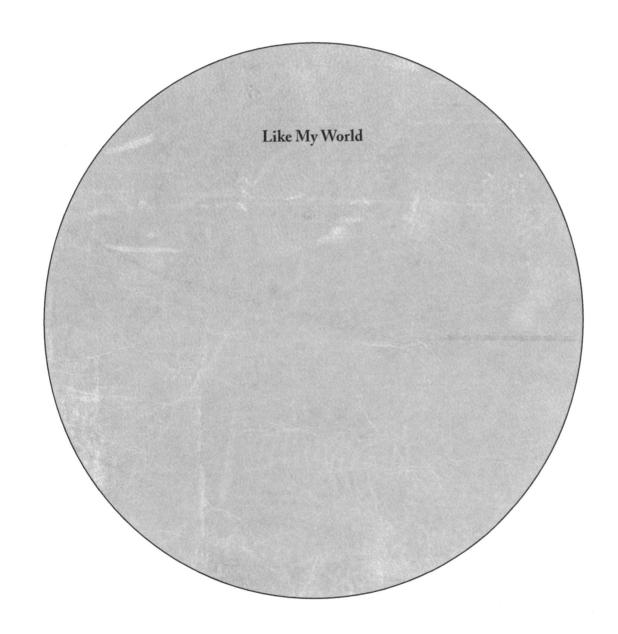

APPENDIX A

Colors of the Canopy Activity with Directions

Colors of the Canopy

1. Find and copy a metaphor or simile.

2. Explain how the metaphor or simile enhances the story's plot, character, or setting.

3. Sensory word or phrase

3. Sensory word or phrase

3. Sensory word or phrase

(Seeing, hearing, touching, smelling, or tasting)

5. Make a prediction about what will happen next in the story.

4. Describe your response to this passage.

6. Copy your favorite sentence or phrase in the passage.

Title:

© 2016, Rita Cevasco & Assoc.

APPENDIX A

Colors of the Canopy Activity

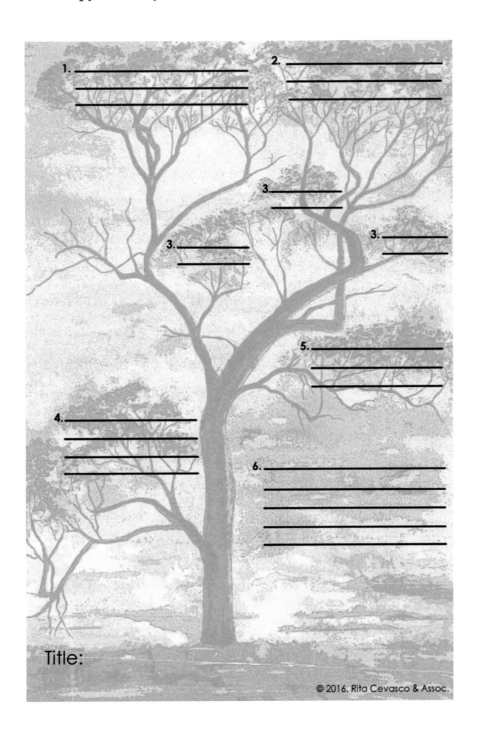

1. _____
   _____
   _____

2. _____
   _____
   _____

3. _____
   _____

3. _____
   _____

3. _____
   _____

5. _____
   _____
   _____

4. _____
   _____
   _____

6. _____
   _____
   _____
   _____
   _____

Title: _____

© 2016. Rita Cevasco & Assoc.

APPENDIX B

Suggested Passages for Children

From *Mercy Watson to the Rescue* by Kate DeCamillo:

This song makes Mercy feel warm inside, as if she has just eaten hot toast with a great deal of butter on it.

Mercy likes hot toast with a great deal of butter on it.

But when Mr. and Mrs. Watson kiss her goodnight and turn off the light, Mercy's room becomes dark.

Very dark.

And Mercy doesn't feel warm and buttery-toasty inside anymore.

From *Bud, Not Buddy* by Christopher Paul Curtis:

I think it's the smell that makes so many folks fall asleep in the library. You'll see someone turn a page and you can imagine a puff of page powder coming up real slow and easy until it starts piling on a person's eyelashes, weighing their eyes down so much they stay down a little longer after each blink and finally making them so heavy that they just don't come back up at all. Then their mouths open and their heads start bouncing up and down like they're bobbing in a big tub of water for apples and before you know it... they're out cold and their face thunks smack-dab on the book.

That's the part that makes librarians the maddest. They get real upset if folks start drooling in the books.

APPENDIX B

Suggested Passages for Children

From *Charlotte's Web* by E.B. White:

On Sunday the church was full. The minister explained the miracle. He said that the words on the spider's web proved that human beings must always be on the watch for the coming of wonders.

All in all, the Zuckermans' pigpen was the center of attraction. Fern was happy, for she felt that Charlotte's trick was working and that Wilber's life would be saved. But she found that the barn was not nearly as pleasant—too many people. She liked it better when she could be all alone with her friends and animals.

From *The Phantom Tollbooth* by Norton Juster:

There was once a boy named Milo who didn't know what to do with himself—not just sometimes, but always.

When he was in school he longed to be out, and when he was out he longed to be in. On the way he thought about coming home, and coming home he thought about going. Wherever he was he wished he were somewhere else, and when he got there he wondered why he'd bothered. Nothing really interested him—least of all the things that should.

APPENDIX B

Suggested Passages for Children

From *Redwall* by Brian Jacques:

Furious with himself, Matthias strode off angrily into the darkening trees. He could find no words strong enough to express his self-contempt. It was not until he had blundered and crashed along his way for some time, wildly upbraiding himself, that he calmed down with the realization that he was well and truly lost. No tree, path or landmark looked remotely familiar. He despaired of ever seeing Redwall again. Night closed in on the small mouse wandering alone in the depths of Mossflower Wood. Strange, imaginary shapes flitted about in the gloom; eerie cries pierced the still air; trees and bushes reached out their branches to catch and scratch like living things with claws. Trembling, Matthias took refuge in an old beech trunk that had once been riven by lightening.

From *To Kill a Mockingbird* by Harper Lee:

Miss Caroline began the day by reading us a story about cats. The cats had long conversations with one another, they wore cunning little clothes and lived in a warm house beneath a kitchen stove. By the time Mrs. Cat called the drugstore for an order of chocolate malted mice the class was wriggling like a bucketful of catawba worms. Miss Caroline seemed unaware that the ragged, denim-shirted and floursack-skirted first grade, most of whom had chopped cotton and fed hogs from the time they were able to walk, were immune to imaginative literature. Miss Caroline came to the end of the story and said, "Oh, my, wasn't that nice?"

APPENDIX B

Suggested Passages for Children

From *Redwall* by Brian Jacques:

The high warm sun shone down on Cluny the Scourge.

Cluny was coming!

He was big, and tough; an evil rat with ragged fur and curved, jagged teeth. He wore a black eye patch; his eye had been torn out in battle with a pike.

Cluny had lost an eye.

The pike had lost its life!

...Cluny was a bilge rat; the biggest, most savage rodent that ever jumped from ship to shore. He was black, with grey and pink scars all over his huge sleek body, from the tip of his wet nose, up past his green and yellow-slitted eye, across both his mean tattered ears, down the length of his heavy vermin-ridden back to the enormous whip-like tail which had earned him his title: Cluny the Scourge!

From *Small Island* by Andrea Levy:

Celia Langley. Celia Langley standing in front of me, her hands on her hips and her head in a cloud. And she is saying: 'Oh, Hortense, when I am older...' All her dreaming began with 'When I am older' '...when I am older, Hortense, I will be leaving Jamaica and I will be going to live in England.' This is when her voice became high-class and her nose point into the air—well, as far as her round nose could—and she swayed as she brought the picture to her mind's eye. 'Hortense, in England I will have a big house with a bell at the front door and I will ring the bell.' And she made the sound, ding-a-ling, ding-a-ling. 'I will ring the bell in this house when I am in England. That is what will happen to me when I am older.'

APPENDIX C

Book Club Samples—On the Page/In my Head

From *The Invention of Wings* by Sue Monk Kidd

On the Page	In My Head - Sample One	In My Head - Sample Two	In My Head - Sample Three
I walked back past the stable and carriage house. The path took me cross the whole map of the world I knew. I hadn't yet seen the spinning globe in the house that showed the rest of it.	Her world limited. Maps she knew was (map she has experienced limited to physical experiences. Had no notion that there was so much more. No reference her world was free of bigger eyes	EVERYONE BELIEVES THEIR LIFE IS NORMAL. EVERYONE LIVES LIKE THEM.	She hasn't seen much of the world but is aware that there's so much more
I poked along, wishing for the day to get used up so me and mauma could go to our room. It sat over the carriage house and didn't have a window. The smell of manure from the stable and the cow house rose up there so ripe it seemed like our bed was stuffed with it instead of straw. The rest of the slaves had their rooms over the kitchen house.	Vision Hetty and mauma in a state of peace, quiet in spite of smells. Nice They had place of respite from their lives. Time alone	AS A KID YOU ALWAYS BELIEVE YOUR LIFE IS GREAT & IT IS HOW THINGS ARE SUPPOSED TO BE. DON'T REALIZE OTHERS HAVE MORE UNTIL OLDER	Used up – how sad I can hardly stop thinking of that expression and how a little girl is using it to describe herself. Manure smell while sleeping – ugh
The wind whipped up and I listened for ship sails snapping in the harbor cross the road, a place I'd smelled on the breeze, but never seen.	Vision ships in the harbor against the blue of sea and sky.		all the senses alert. I can hear the wind & smell it. Think I can see it
The sails would go off like whips cracking and all us would listen to see was it some slave getting flogged in a neighbor-yard or was it ships making ready to leave. You found out when the screams started up or not.	Shiver thinking of what slaves were experiencing. Hear the screams. Almost feel them. Feel for them (slaves) That they lived through this That this was their existence	HARD TO BELIEVE SOMEONE COULD THINK A GOOD SOUND WAS SOMETHING BAD	The visual of slaves getting whipped makes me taste blood in my mouth
The sun had gone, leaving a puckered place in the clouds, like the button had fallen off. I picked up the battling stick by the wash pot, and for no good reason, jabbed it into a squash in the vegetable garden. I pitched the butternut over the wall where it splatted in a loud mess.	Vision a beautiful sunset.	SEE SOMEONE FIST CLENCHED WITH SOMETHING TO DO DOING SOMETHING TO KEEP FROM SCREAMING	The imagery of the sky as an unbuttoned blouse - lovely. But she's angry and throws the squash. I'm angry too
Then the air turned still. Missus' voice came from the back door, said, "Aunt-Sister, bring Hetty in here to me right now."	Oh no...What does she want. Treat her well Vision Missus yelling	UH - OH	Stop in my track Fear of what will happen
I went to the house, thinking she was in an uproar over her squash. I told my backside to brace up.	Vision Hetty tensing up. Bracing for punishment.	I'M IN TROUBLE NOW	I can feel her fear, see it in the description of her back stiffening.

APPENDIX C

Student Samples—Reading with a Pencil

From *Little Women* by Louisa May Alcott

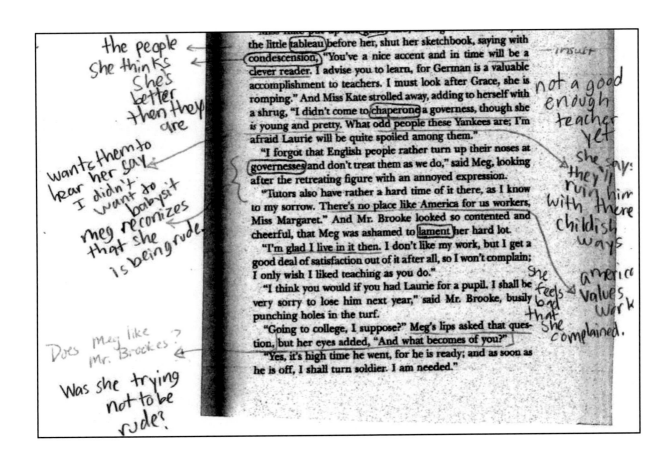

APPENDIX C

Student Samples—On the Page/In my Head

From *The City of Ember* by Jeanne DuPrau

The City Of Ember

PASSAGE	In my head
It was like finding yourself on a deadend street, Lina thought.	doesn't know were to go
She stared blankly at the things that had once been her daily compinions— the teachers desk, the stacks of paper, The book of the City of ember on its special shelf	remembering happy times, She doesn't like the book because it's not all true
The old words ran in her head: "there is no place but Ember."	She was mabe told this s, flei wouln't ascape.
"Ember is the only light in the dark world."	She knows theres a nother place
She knew know that this wasn't true. There was some place else—the place were the boats would take them.	She is probably feeling angry because shes been lied to her whole life
	⇓
	Prediction: mayor might be the cause of this.

APPENDIX C

Student Samples—Cartooning Characters

From *Rebecca* by Daphne Du Maurier

Character: Mrs. de Winter, in conversation

"I know people are looking me up and down, wondering what sort of success I'm going to make of it. I can imagine them saying, 'What on earth does Maxim see in her?' and I begin to doubt, and I have a fearful haunting feeling that I should never have married Maxim, that we are not going to be happy."

Mrs. de Winter by Moira Cevasco, age 14

About Rita Cevasco

I am a Speech Language Pathologist, specializing in reading and writing, and a mom. I was a therapist before I became a mom and throughout my homeschool years. Now, more than thirty years later, I still provide therapy in my private practice in Mason, Ohio while acting as an on-call mom to my adult children. My mom-brain/therapist-brain is so entwined it is hard to know which gray cells belong where!

After additional training in both dyslexia and dysgraphia, I developed online classes for Brave Writer, authored the *Wand*, and continually create new ideas for teaching reading and writing. I train tutors, consult with Brave Writer, and work directly with children of all ages who struggle with reading and writing, and with the parents who struggle at their sides. You can visit RootedinLanguage.com to read my blog for more ideas on growing readers and writers.

About Tracy Molitors

Despite drawing and painting all my life, I was well into adulthood before I could say aloud, *"I am an artist."* With the encouragement of my husband, kids, and friends, I have entered competitions, learned new media, and taught children and adults to find their inner artists. I enjoy taking complex ideas (especially about art and reading) and making them Visible and Enjoyable. My love of teaching children, art, and storytelling combine within the realm of children's books and illustration. Nothing is more satisfying than engaging the imagination of a child! You can visit me at TracyMolitors.com to see more of my work or ConnectingArtToLanguageArts.com to read my blog.

Many thanks...

To Laurie, Nemo, and Sigourney, we can't thank you enough for your generosity and courage in opening up your experiences for all to share.

To Julie Bogart, the bravest person I know! You are a woman of vision, and we are grateful to be a part of your complex and ever-expanding web.

With much appreciation for professional contributions and inspiration from the following people: Michelle Fill, MS, SLP; Donna Ridley, M.Ed., SLP; Moira Chrzanowski, MA, SLP; and countless other language and reading experts.

Special thanks to Nancy Graham for your tireless editing, expertise, and encouragement. And to Claire Molitors for sharing your time and talent as our beta reader and first round editor. We are grateful to you both for respecting our vision, then helping us communicate it clearly.

Thanks to Tom Molitors for your computer know-how and patient problem-solving expertise, especially when technology developed a mind of its own.

Thank you Vincent Cevasco for wrestling the social media monkey, and researching new and mysterious tools unfamiliar to us.

More Thanks from Rita...

To my parents and siblings for teaching me to love the library, and for always encouraging my writing—especially Jodi Weber for her endless enthusiasm and inspiration.

With gratitude to my amazing husband, Rick: you fill my cup each day, in endless ways. We labor and play together in every arena.

Still More Thanks from Tracy...

To my parents and siblings for creating a home where all read-alouds were theatre and all art was encouraged. Thanks for the great education in art, music, books, and family.

And always to Tom whose endless support includes deep knowledge, useful skills, and the willingness to provide the engineering for an art project at a moment's notice!

Made in the USA
Monee, IL
10 July 2024

61614609R00090